# Franklin County
# Ghosts
# of Pennsylvania

To Melanie –
Thanks for coming to
hear all this! Enjoy
the stories and don't be
afraid! Γεια σας (God Bless!)
Athena Varo 10/30/09

# Athena Varounis

4880 Lower Valley Road, Atglen, Pennsylvania 19310

**Other Schiffer Books on Related Subjects**
*Pennsylvania's Adams County Ghosts*, 978-0-7643-3123-7, $14.99
*Philly's Main Line Haunts*, 978-0-7643-3181-7, $14.99
*Ghosts of West Chester*, Pennsylvania, 978-0-7643-2996-8, $14.99

Schiffer Books are available at special discounts for bulk purchases for sales promotions or premiums. Special editions, including personalized covers, corporate imprints, and excerpts can be created in large quantities for special needs. For more information contact the publisher:

Schiffer Publishing Ltd.
4880 Lower Valley Road
Atglen, PA 19310
Phone: (610) 593-1777
Fax: (610) 593-2002
E-mail: Info@schifferbooks.com

For the largest selection of fine reference books on this and related subjects, please visit our web site at: **www.schifferbooks.com** We are always looking for people to write books on new and related subjects. If you have an idea for a book please contact us at the above address.

This book may be purchased from the publisher. Include $5.00 for shipping. Please try your bookstore first. You may write for a free catalog.

In Europe, Schiffer books are distributed by
Bushwood Books
6 Marksbury Ave.
Kew Gardens
Surrey TW9 4JF England
Phone: 44 (0) 20 8392 8585; Fax: 44 (0) 20 8392 9876
E-mail: info@bushwoodbooks.co.uk
Website: www.bushwoodbooks.co.uk

Designed by Stephanie Daugherty
Type set in Batik Regular/AmericanTypewriter Medium/NewBskvll BT

ISBN: 978-0-7643-3257-9
Printed in China

# Dedication

*This book is dedicated to Friederike "Rickey" Kolbay,
a teacher, mentor, and friend.*

I will not espalier your soul
on the trellis of my needs;
will not prune your inclinations
to suit my limitations.
I'd rather be surprised,
delighted at the unexpected
unfolding of leaf or flower,
of something somewhere unanticipated:
newly you unfurled,
rather than a reflection
of my own expectation.

-- Rickey Kolbay

# Acknowledgments

No significant accomplishment is achieved in solitude. Without the unqualified support, enthusiasm, and dedication of the following individuals, this endeavor would not have succeeded:

➤ Deborah M. Heinecker was living in peaceful anonymity when I enticed her out of "retirement" and requested her collaboration on this project. Deborah's psychic gifts provided unique insights and rich details to the apparitions discovered in the locations we explored. Unselfishly devoting countless hours bringing these stories to life, nothing presented in the pages that follow would have been possible without her.

➤ Michael J. Albert's extensive historical research provided a solid factual core to the legends. He tirelessly escorted me to numerous haunted sites made available by the Franklin County Historical Society-Kittochtinny and facilitated much of the access to Wilson College.

➤ Marie Lanser Beck's unfailing faith in my ability to write carried me through my darkest doubts. My own personal cheering section, Marie edited and proofread my words and spurred me on to the finish.

➤ And no ghost story can be told without the cooperation of the haunted. There are many people in Franklin County who made this volume possible by sharing their experiences, gathering information, and granting me access to private homes and public venues. I am especially grateful for the invaluable assistance provided by Bonnie Iseminger, Renfrew Museum and Park, Waynesboro; Ann Hull, Franklin County Historical Society-Kittochtinny, Chambersburg; Bonnie A. Shockey, Allison-Antrim Museum, Greencastle; and Linda A. Boeckman, Capitol Theater, Chambersburg.

# Contents

# Foreword

Not everyone is wild about history, but everyone *loves* ghost stories—believers and non-believers alike. It's all about that little shudder that goes up your spine at the notion of the unseen presence, or the intellectual riddle of "what if" that makes the stories of the supernatural so fascinating.

In this collection of ghost stories from Franklin County, Pennsylvania, Athena Varounis has unlocked not only a door to the psychic world, but uncovered a back door to history—specifically local history. In the skillful recounting of eerie encounters and ghostly experiences never before captured in print, she introduces us to the events and personalities that have shaped our communities. Her investigation not only expands inquiry into the paranormal, but also spurs the quest for what may prove even more elusive—historical fact.

From her account of the ghoulish post-burial trials of Revolutionary War hero and Waynesboro namesake "Mad" Anthony Wayne to the question asked by generations of Penn State Mont Alto students: "Who haunts Wiestling Hall?" to the cause of the mysterious flickering lights seen along the East Branch of the Antietam Creek, the quest for the historical foundation for local ghost stories reveals much about our endangered past.

These ghost stories may or may not shed light into an ethereal dimension that equal numbers of believers and skeptics embrace or dismiss—for the telling of what cannot be seen is truly in the eye of the believer. But these manifestations of long ago energy, whether embedded in limestone or simply in folklore, are an enduring curiosity. These stories will not only send you rummaging for that misplaced nightlight, but may actually prompt you to dig more deeply into Franklin County's rich historical legacy of Indian raids, frontier farmers, Civil War soldiers, storekeepers, and visionaries.

Proceed with caution... These tales may give you second thoughts about driving through Pond Bank late at night, and dissuade you from visiting the basement of Chambersburg's Old Jail, or lingering at the Capitol Theatre after hours. But if these stories make you rush to the dusty pages of *The History of Franklin County,* or track down accounts of the reputed massacre of the Renfrew sisters, beware. As intriguing as ghosts may be, the reality you uncover may prove even more captivating.

-- *Marie Lanser Beck*

# Introduction

The beauty of a ghost story is that it can be anything the reader wants it to be. The sound of footsteps in empty hallways, lights turning themselves on and off, doors opening and closing on their own, the occasional sound of voices or music, unexpected scents, and the very rare glimpse of an apparition can be irrefutable proof to one and irrelevant to another that entities are indeed amongst us.

Since the beginning of recorded history, all cultures have had ghost stories, and, since the very first story, all cultures have been trying to define what ghosts are. Rosemary Ellen Guiley, in her *Encyclopedia of Ghosts and Spirits*, defines a ghost as "an alleged spirit of the dead." This is the most common view. Some researchers or "paranormal investigators" theorize that ghosts are a type of human or animal energy imprinted upon the environment as the result of a traumatic emotional event. These energies, stored by inexplicable means, are experienced when environmental factors cause their release. Still others believe ghosts are glimpses into other dimensions or times, perceived through porous borders where worlds bleed over into the past, present, and future.

The ghost stories you are about to enjoy might lead you to accept any one of these theories—or none of them. You are welcome to develop your own interpretations and explanations of the phenomena unfolding before you. Although Guiley and other paranormal researchers define the terms "apparition" and "entity" as separate types or manifestations of ghosts, for the purpose of the stories you are about to explore, they can be considered one and the same: A ghost is a ghost, and/or an apparition, and/or an entity.

One unique aspect to the tales that follow, which sets them apart from others you might have read, is that these ghost stories are a combination of historical research, interviews, objective investigation, and psychic impressions.

I conducted the research into the legends with the same investigative clarity required in my twenty-four years as an FBI Agent. Once a location seemed suitable for further study, my colleague and collaborator, Deborah M. Heinecker, returned with me and provided information obtained through her unique psychic abilities—making the past all the more chillingly real.

The "Apparitions" portion of each tale reveals the entities and events perceived at each location. The last story in this book, "Mont Alto," reveals exactly how we did it.

But please, enjoy these stories as the entertainment they are meant to be. Stop in where invited as you take a haunted journey across Franklin County through private homes and public establishments. The ghosts are eagerly anticipating your arrival.

# 1

# Wilson College

**1015 Philadelphia Avenue,
Chambersburg, Pennsylvania**

## Riddle Hall

**S**he grabbed the knob and slammed the door behind her as she fled the room. She did not care that everyone on the third floor would hear the sound. It was 1 a.m. on a Friday night and chances were not many of her dorm mates were sleeping. She ran down the hallway and threw open the metal fire door to the stairwell.

She wondered if *it* would...come after her. Could she feel it? Was it at her back, breathing on her hair, just ready to... *No*, don't look back! Keep going!

She held onto the banister, fearful that her momentum would cause her to fall down the steps. This could not be happening. Was it behind her? She rounded the second floor landing and almost knocked over a classmate who was coming up the stairs.

She did not hear the classmate ask her what was wrong or where was she going. She just kept moving. Down to the first floor, through the fire doors, through the lobby, and out the door into the night.

The cold air slapped her right in the face. Although a senior at Wilson College, like most of her colleagues in October 1975, she did not own a car. She went around to the side of the dorm where the bicycles stood lined up in their stanchions, found hers, and took off down the drive. The shadow of the dormitory grew smaller behind her as the trees and the greenery flew by her in the dark. She sped out onto Pennsylvania Avenue, the main street that hemmed the campus on the east side.

Chambersburg still enforced a curfew for all individuals under the age of twenty-one, requiring that they be accompanied by an adult or off the streets by 11 p.m. So she stuck to the sidewalks and side streets and kept the light on her bike turned off, finding her way instead by streetlight and porch light and hiding in alleys when a suspected police car came by. Finally she made it to the building

that housed the *Public Opinion*, the local newspaper that employed her as an intern.

A few lights were on in the offices and pressroom where the night shift toiled on deadlines and layouts. She used her keys to get in and quietly made her way to her desk, a small, cluttered space in the corner of a large, desk-filled cluttered room.

She cradled her face in her hands and sat there in the dark, struggling to catch her breath. Okay, you're safe now, she said to herself, calm down and stop shaking. *It* hadn't followed her...*it* wasn't here. It couldn't be here. *It* was still locked up in her room—on the third floor of Riddle Hall—on the Wilson College campus.

They would find her at her desk in the morning, head resting on her arms, sound asleep. She would never spend another night in Riddle.

Their friends would think she was crazy. *No one* moved out of Riddle. Riddle was the dormitory *everyone* wanted to live in. But she would have them both moved by the time her roommate returned on Sunday night. She would think up something to tell her. They would move to Prentis Hall, a dormitory across the campus, far away from Riddle. After that weekend, she would never enter the room on the third floor of Riddle again.

## Room Drawing

It had all started innocuously enough. In the 1970s, years before personal computers, digital music devices, and cellular telephones, room selection at Wilson College was conducted on a lottery system. Numbers were written on slips of paper and drawn in the spring for the selection of rooms in September. Annette had drawn number seven. "That's low enough to get us into Riddle!" her friend Rachel had exclaimed. They had gotten to know one another freshmen year,

**Riddle Hall, Wilson College.**

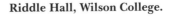

Portrait of Henry A. Riddle, located in the Riddle Hall parlor.

became friends almost immediately, and planned to room together senior year. Residency in Riddle, because it was the most popular dormitory on campus, required two to a room at the time of room drawing and because they had first pick in room drawing, Riddle was primarily a senior dorm.

The Henry Alexander Riddle Memorial Hall was dedicated in June 1928 and named for Wilson College Trustee, Henry A. Riddle. Riddle had been on the Wilson College Board of Trustees for some thirty years when he died in his home in Chambersburg on October 6, 1924. Riddle's daughter, Elisabeth Riddle, Wilson College Class of 1897, served as the Hostess to the College and Assistant to the Dean at the time of the dormitory's dedication.

Riddle Hall was constructed during a time of prosperity and growth for Wilson College in the post World War I years and came about as the result of generous alumnae contributions. Built of native limestone, the Gothic Revival three-story dormitory is located on the southeastern edge of the main campus. The dormitory, designed with suites in which two rooms share a connecting bathroom, can house up to sixty students.

With its maple furnishing, interior oak woodwork, and beautiful lounge, Riddle had been the dormitory of choice for Wilson's wealthier students back in the days when social status was a factor in college life, but this tradition gradually faded and by the 1970s none of the Wilson students knew that it had ever even existed. The women of this era sought no personal recognition based on where they lived on campus; rather, they desired Riddle for its rooms and bathrooms. The rooms were private and sharing a bathroom with three other women at the most was immensely more desirable than sharing what was basically a large, public restroom with all of the women on a particular floor.

Annette and Rachel selected a room on the third floor overlooking the Wilson College green. Their suitemates would be two other seniors whom they knew and liked.

At the end of the school year, students packed their belongings and put them into cardboard boxes marked with their names and new room numbers. The boxes were moved into storage by college staff over the summer. When Annette and Rachel returned to the campus in the fall of 1975 and went up to their room in Riddle, their boxes were already there.

But as they unpacked, they were both surprised to see the condition their boxes were in. Some of the tape had been ripped

At Riddle Hall, the uppermost windows are to Annette's room.

off. While nothing inside had been disturbed and nothing had been taken, the boxes bore deep scratches and odd scuffs. "It looks like something was chewing on them," Rachel said. Annette shuddered unexpectedly, suddenly cold. The frigid air had come from nowhere. It was early September in Pennsylvania, the room was hot and stuffy, and they had opened all the windows to let in some air. "Probably mice," Annette said, shivering, even though she did not believe mice could make such long, deep, perfectly placed gouges. "If it *was* a mouse," Rachel replied, "I'd hate to see the size of it!"

## *Not Mice*

It was Annette's habit to sit up in her bed at night and read by the light of a lamp situated on the dresser beside her bed. She usually stayed up late while Rachel went to sleep early. Annette was very quiet and the light didn't bother Rachel. It seemed Rachel could sleep through anything. It was all working out well.

Annette had gotten used to the sounds of Riddle. Floors creaked, steam pipes banged, and footsteps were magnified on the wide, wooden floors of the hallways. Even soft voices carried, and you always knew when the person living next to you was in their room. It was a pretty drafty place, too, with large gaps under the old, wooden doors and some sort of wind always whistling in the hallway, especially at night when doors down the hall opened and closed.

She couldn't remember when the tapping began. Faint at first, becoming more deliberate as the evenings passed, something tapped the plaster inside the wall by her bed.

"Do you hear that tapping?" she asked Rachel one night when the sound seemed unusually loud.

"What tapping?" Rachel replied as she got into bed.

"There's a tapping sound coming from inside the wall here by my bed."

"I don't hear anything. Besides, it's probably mice. The same mice that ate our boxes."

It's not mice, Annette thought. She did not bring it up again.

Then there was the cold spot by the bathroom door. "Don't you feel that?" Annette asked every time she walked into it. It was unpredictable, as if some unseen freezer door would open, releasing a blast of arctic breath across the threshold.

"No," Rachel replied every time, "I don't feel anything."

After a while, she stopped mentioning this as well.

And she never even brought up the fact that sometimes in the morning her pen would not be on her desk where she had left it, but had somehow moved to the window sill...or that her books sometimes fell off her desk while they were in class, as she would often find them on the floor. And there were other things that she had begun to notice, but would not mention...like the feeling she was being watched when she was in the bathroom.

## Stories...

There had always been stories about Riddle. The old dorm had charm, but there was something dark and foreboding about it as well, particularly at night, when the atmosphere inside seemed to change. Throughout the years, the young women who lived there spoke of phantom footsteps on all of the floors, doors opening and closing on their own, and overhead lights turning on and off. The television lounge was in the basement and on more than one occasion, the women gathered there to watch a late night show were disturbed by the loud steps of someone running down the back stairway. They watched the stairway expecting to see the frantic runner, but no one appeared.

In one particular room on the first floor, students living there in different years consistently complained of returning to the room at various times to find the dresser drawers open and their clothing disturbed.

In another room on the third floor, down the hall from where Annette was having her problems, the sound of someone pounding on the door at around 2 a.m. intermittently disturbed the sleep of students living in that room. But no one ever saw anyone knock and no one claimed responsibility. Once a young woman opened the door as it was still shaking from being pounded with what seemed like a solid fist, only to be greeted by the dark, empty hallway on the other side.

The connecting bathroom between Annette's and the adjoining room
in Riddle Hall.

Women studying in the lobby at night would hear voices coming from a small room just off the main floor where chaperones allegedly sat while Wilson College students of an earlier era entertained male guests. Upon inspection, the room was always empty. At other times, students would look up at the sound of footsteps entering the lobby from the front door, only to see no one. And they would watch in curiosity or fear as the steps of the *invisible* guest walked around them to the chaperone room.

There had always been stories about Riddle, but Annette had never heard anything about the room she was in and she likely would not have paid any attention if she had. It wasn't until many years later that she found out everything that had happened to her had happened to others—in classes before her and classes that came after—but in October of 1975, she did not know this. Nor did she know the worst was yet to come...

## Windows

The windows were always open. Annette did not notice this for weeks, not until it began to get colder as the Pennsylvania autumn descended and the days grew shorter and darker. Just like the tapping, the matter of the windows began softly, barely noticeable, and evolved into a source of conflict that almost destroyed the roommates' friendship...as if the room had begun to turn on them, marshalling all of its elements for a frontal assault on happiness it could not tolerate.

Annette woke up shivering. She had closed and latched the heavy windows when she went to bed. Rachel had come in uncharacteristically late and had gone to bed after her. Now it was three in the morning and the cold breeze was tossing their curtains back against the walls and flooding over Annette like a dry cold shower. The fully opened casement windows sucked in the crisp, biting air from the Wilson College green. An unfamiliar current she knew was anger invaded her thoughts. She got out of bed, reached for the handles on the windows, and pulled them in quietly, locking them shut.

In the morning they would be wide open again.

And it just kept happening.

**Window in Riddle Hall with Norland Hall in the background.**

**Latch on window in Riddle Hall.**

Finally, she said something. "Rachel, I know you don't get as cold as I do, but I'd really appreciate it if you wouldn't open all the windows at night."

"I'm not opening the windows," Rachel replied sharply.

Annette was astonished by Rachel's tone. "Well, yes you have. I close them when I go to bed and in the morning, they're always open. It's just that it's getting colder and I..."

"Annette, I'm not opening the windows," Rachel cut her off. "I've been cold, too. I thought *you* were opening them."

Annette shook her head. "No, I keep closing them."

"Well, maybe you don't close them right and the wind just blows them open," Rachel said. "You have to turn the handle down, make sure it locks in place."

Annette knew how to close and lock the windows. She began to respond, but stopped herself.

As October passed by, the windows became more and more of an issue. It got to the point where Annette was hesitant to glance up at her room between classes, fearing she'd be taunted by the gaping frames of open windows.

## *Dreams*

It was all beginning to wear on her. She did not know why Rachel did not react to the situation the way she did. Rachel just seemed to ignore everything, or not even feel it. Rachel never complained about the cold by the bathroom door and never mentioned anything about items in the room being disturbed or moved. They had both ceased to address the windows. Annette rarely slept through the night now as she was often awakened by a sound, the windows, and especially, lately, what she thought was a touch. Rachel just seemed to go about her business as Annette descended into exhaustion and their warm friendship fragmented into strained civility.

She began to dream on a regular basis that she was in the room alone at night and a female presence watched her from the dark by the casement windows. After a while she couldn't tell whether she was dreaming or feeling the presence just before awakening. Often she lay there, pretending to sleep, sensing that the woman was standing at the foot of her bed, watching her. She would lay still and wait for the woman to leave. It became a strange, sick game, playing out in her mind.

Other nights, she thought she felt a touch. If she fell asleep on her stomach, she would be awakened by pressure in the middle of her back, like a hand pressing her into the mattress. Annette would bolt awake, gasping for air as if her breathing had been obstructed.

Through it all, she went to class, she studied in the library, and told no one about the *presence* in her room. If she had, if Annette had told her suitemates what she was hearing, feeling, and seeing, and that the windows kept opening of their own accord, she would have discovered that the women next door were going through their own disconcerting experiences in a room they thought they would love.

Both of them had seen shadows zigzag across their room, like graphite lightening bolts. One had appeared in the threshold of the bathroom one night and disappeared into Annette's room. They never told her.

Items on their dressers moved on their own and posters peeled off the walls.

And the windows, the casement windows they always locked shut, would somehow fly open.

### THE DREAM

Rachel announced she would be going home for a "long weekend," a scheduled break over a weekend in October that coincided with the Columbus Day holiday. Rachel had left around noon that Friday, cutting a few classes to get a head start. Annette wouldn't be going anywhere as she had been given a newspaper assignment on Saturday.

It was approaching 11 p.m. and she was tired. She had been reading for about an hour, propped up against some pillows in bed, the lamp on her dresser casting a soft, dim light across her book. Music filtered in through the wall from her next-door neighbor's radio. She heard no tapping tonight and the windows... were shut. The room felt uncannily calm. Annette put her book away and turned off the light. She fell asleep in minutes.

**Warfield Hall, Wilson College.**

She dreamt she was sitting in her German class, in a classroom in Warfield Hall. All of her classmates were there, and the professor, Herr Kellinger, was speaking. Suddenly, a force she could not see lifted her from her desk and threw her on her back onto the hard wooden floor. She could not move. She lay there, looking up at the faces of everyone in the room, now surrounding her in a circle.

An invisible weight pinned her down and she was totally paralyzed. Darkness began to expand behind the people watching her. As it grew larger, wiping out the background, she looked up at

the ceiling and saw that the room was collapsing inward as the floor began to buckle beneath her.

She knew she was dreaming, but she could not wake up. Everything began to crumble. As the floor sank further and further away from the classroom, she felt a vacuum sucking her down into darkness, pressure increasing against her chest, compressing her body so that she could not breathe.

*Wake up!* She demanded, but she could not pull out of it. The sound of destruction, of wood collapsing, of plaster walls crumbling, blasted her ears. As she fell further and further into the void, gasping for breath, she latched onto a melody lurking behind the destruction. Music! A song coming from the radio in the room next door!

She seized upon the notes and envisioned them knotted together in a thin, undulating rope that she mentally climbed, as she still could not move.

*Wake up!* She demanded.

She bolted upright in her bed, sucking in air. A split second later, essentially simultaneous with the realization that she was awake, she watched in horror as the handles on the cast iron windows unlatched themselves and the windows flew open.

That was it... She threw on her clothes and fled the room.

# Epilogue

Riddle Hall remains one of the most popular dormitories on the Wilson College campus. Throughout the old, majestic building, lights still go on and off and footsteps still begin and end in empty hallways and empty rooms and on the back stairway. No one knows how many young women have come and gone from the two rooms in question over the years as no such records have ever been kept. Students still complain of posters and pictures peeling back or falling off the walls in the third floor suite and maintenance has been called more than once regarding suspected mice in a wall where tapping sounds emanate at night. The handles on the casement windows there have been oiled, cleaned, and inspected countless times based on complaints that the metal seems to have a mind of its own, unlocking repeatedly to open windows absent human touch.

Riddle is one of the dormitories used to house guests attending conventions and other activities that the college hosts

**Riddle Hall.**

over the summer months. Michael J. Albert, the former Facilities and Plant Manager for Wilson College, recalled an incident in the summer of 2007 when he was paged late one night to respond to a woman's complaint in a room on the third floor of Riddle. "They told me there was a problem in Riddle," Michael said. "They gave me no details. Just, can you come over and talk to this lady?"

Michael went over to Riddle and knocked on the door to the room. "A lady opens the door and I said, 'I was told there was a problem.'"

The woman appeared to be in her 60s and quite lucid. She directed Michael into the room and pointed to an old, cherry dresser that had been there for decades. It was the same dresser Annette had used during her short stay. "There's a ghost in that dresser," the woman said matter-of-factly.

Michael looked at her. "Pardon?"

"Honest," the woman replied, "I can smell it. It smells like death. There's a ghost in that dresser. I can't sleep in this room tonight with that dresser in here."

Michael did not smell anything. "What do you want me to do?" he asked.

"Just move it out into the hall."

Michael pushed the heavy dresser out into the hallway. "Is this good enough?" he asked.

"Yes," the woman said. "I'll be able to sleep tonight."

The next day the woman was gone and Michael pushed the dresser back into the room.

All of the furniture in Riddle has since been replaced. "I have no idea where that dresser is today," Michael said. "It could be in storage. Or someone could have taken it." Michael shrugged. "It's probably sitting in someone's house."

# Wilson Female College

Wilson College was conceived in the summer of 1867 when the Reverend James W. Wightman, pastor of Greencastle Presbyterian Church, and Dr. Tyron Edwards, pastor of Hagerstown Presbyterian Church, decided that women should be afforded the same higher educational opportunities as men. In order to establish their idea of the ideal women's college, they had to raise enough money, find a site, advertise the college, and recruit students, none of which was a minimal endeavor during an era in which women were essentially viewed as chattel.

The Reverends Wightman and Edwards focused on Chambersburg as the site for the college and began to solicit support in the way of monetary contributions and pledges.

During the fall and winter of 1867, after many trips to the town, they managed to enlist the support of a group of prominent men who later became Wilson's first Board of Trustees.

Then, in the spring of 1868, Reverend Edwards decided to approach Sarah Wilson and ask for a cash donation. Sarah was the last surviving member of a large family that had accumulated twenty-four farms in St. Thomas Township. Upon the death of her brother in 1867, Sarah inherited an aggregate estate worth $400,000. She contributed $30,000 in cash to be used toward the founding of the college.

Wilson's co-founders submitted plans for the college to the Carlisle Presbytery and received its endorsement in April 1868, but a charter from the Commonwealth of Pennsylvania could not be pursued until an actual location for the college was established.

The citizens of Chambersburg were complacent in their financial support of the college. When it appeared adequate funds would not be raised there, the newly appointed

**The Norland Mansion, which became part of Wilson College as Norland Hall.**

Board of Trustees announced to the towns comprising Franklin County that whichever town pledged the most money would be chosen as the site of the college. It wasn't until another town put up $16,000 that Chambersburg rose to the challenge and produced $23,000, "earning" the right to be chosen as the site for the college.

One of the most magnificent properties in Chambersburg was Norland Farm, the homestead of Colonel Alexander K. McClure. McClure (1828-1909), owner and editor of the local newspaper, was a state legislator, and vehement opponent of slavery. A Republican

Party powerbroker, McClure was instrumental in Pennsylvania's support for Lincoln in the 1864 election.

McClure's house and farm buildings were burned in retribution when Confederate soldiers, under the command of Colonel John McCausland, set fire to the town of Chambersburg July 30, 1864. After the war, McClure spent more than $20,000 to rebuild Norland, a four-story Victorian structure, making it the finest mansion in the area.

The house and grounds were up for sale in October 1868, as McClure planned to move to Philadelphia where he would become editor of *The Philadelphia Times*. The site provided the ideal location for the proposed women's college, but McClure wanted more money for the property than the founders anticipated, so Reverend Edwards, along with other trustees, paid another visit to Sarah Wilson. In October 1868, Sarah pledged an additional $20,000 on the condition that the "college should stand as a memorial of herself and her family."

On March 9, 1869, the deed to Norland Farm was transferred and Wilson College had a home. The Pennsylvania legislature issued a charter on March 24, 1869, naming the new institution Wilson Female College in honor of Sarah Wilson. Eventually renamed Wilson College, instruction began on October 12, 1870.

## Norland Hall

Norland Hall, the signature building of Wilson College, with its stately arches and mansard roof, stands very much today, at least in exterior appearance, as it did when the college was born. Through the years it has served as a classroom building, dormitory, and office building. Currently the white Victorian structure contains apartments and guest rooms on the upper floors that house faculty and visitors, and a few remaining guest rooms on the second floor share space with offices and conference rooms. The

Norland Hall, Wilson College.

magnificent parlor on the main floor remains intact, however, offices located in the adjoining rooms have marred its splendor with modern clutter. Although extensive reconfiguration of the interior has been necessary to accommodate modern fire codes and needed office space, some of the floors and rooms remain untouched. It is in these rooms, where the walls, ceilings, and floors have been spared rebirth that...*energy* can be sensed...and from which stories unfold of footsteps, apparitions, and faucets that misbehave.

There is a legend that has been repeated through the years by alumnae, staff, and faculty, telling the sad tale of McClure's daughter and her love for a wounded Confederate soldier she kept hidden in Norland's attic. The Confederate soldier, reportedly wounded in Gettysburg, had collapsed in the woods near Norland farm and was discovered by McClure's daughter. She enlisted the help of servants and hid the man in the attic. Knowing that her father would have the man executed or sent to a prisoner of war camp, McClure's daughter tended to the man's wounds in secret. As she nursed him back to health, they fell in love and made plans to be together when the war ended.

As is usually the case with such legends, McClure discovered his daughter's lover. After banishing his daughter to some undisclosed location, McClure allegedly boarded the poor soldier up in the attic and left him there to die. It's been said that the footsteps heard in Norland's attic are those of this poor soldier trying to find a way out, and that the moans and cries drifting down from the stairs at night are his desperate pleas for mercy.

Some Wilson College students from the 1960s and early 1970s have claimed that during a history seminar held in one of the rooms on the third floor, a student was suddenly "possessed" — and began to write in elegant Cooperplate script the soldier's story. The woman remained in a "trance" until she finished writing and then collapsed. Sent to the college infirmary, her parents removed her from the school and she was never heard from again.

Students staying on campus between semesters have conducted forays into Norland's attic in search of the ghost of the Confederate soldier. Some believe they have felt or seen him there in the shadows. They seek to comfort the poor soldier and McClure's daughter, pitying the hopelessness of their forbidden love.

**Main staircase, Norland Hall.**

However popular this legend might be, McClure did not have a daughter, and Norland, like much of the town of Chambersburg, was burned to the ground July 30, 1864.

Faculty members renting an apartment on the third floor have consistently complained about the cold water in the bathroom sink faucet suddenly turning on by itself at various times of the day and night. Washers and hardware have been replaced numerous times, but the problem persists.

In other apartments and in some offices, malfunctioning lights and electrical items are constant sources of irritation for residents and for the maintenance workers repeatedly called to remedy perplexing problems.

A huge bedroom suite on the second floor was once the most popular guest room on campus. Distinguished guests of the college were always placed there and sometimes parents who visited at the right time were able to reserve the elegant room.

Scores of people have spent the night in this bedroom without incident. Others, however, have endured sleepless nights in various stages of fear, wondering what was tapping at the window and listening to the sound of footsteps pacing in the hallway.

Acclaimed pianist Lilian Kraus, a fearless prodigy who fled Europe a step ahead of the Nazis, performed a concert at Wilson College in the 1970s. When shown the grand bedroom suite on the second floor of Norland where she would be staying, Kraus refused to enter the room. "I am not staying here," she is reported to have said, turning away from the door. She ended up at a motel in town, refusing to stay anywhere on the Wilson College campus.

Mamie Doud Eisenhower, wife of the 34th President of the United States, Dwight D. Eisenhower, had been a guest of the college sometime during the 1960s. She allegedly fled the room in the middle of the night with no explanation given.

The bedroom suite has since been dissected, part of it lopped off to form an office. But the main sleeping area remains intact and overnight guests still complain from time to time about footsteps in the hallway at night, just outside the door, or sleep interrupted by unexplained tapping on antique window panes.

Norland was present at Wilson's birth and has witnessed every day in the life of the college. It remains to be discovered who actually wanders the attic and the source of the otherworldly cries heard by guests and residents remains unknown. Whatever paces the hallway outside the second floor bedroom never walks down to the first floor and never goes back upstairs. It's likely that this phenomenon is related in some way to the tapping on the windows in the room, but no one can say for sure. The faucet in the apartment continues to turn itself on and electronic devices continue to flicker.

The entities in Norland remain there to this day, inside, behind the antique windows with bubbles in the glass, the old, white mansion regally watching over the campus in deceptive silence.

## Sarah Wilson's Portrait

A portrait of Sarah Wilson hangs in the dining hall, over a sealed fireplace, just at the entrance to the kitchen. The painting previously hung in Patterson Lounge, but sometime during the recent past made its way into the dining hall. As soon as the portrait appeared there, a rumor began to circulate that one should never remove the painting or cover it. Sarah seemed to like the dining hall, where she could see all of the students every day and know that her donations to establish the college had been worthwhile.

During the summer months, the dining hall in Wilson College can be rented for events, such as meetings, special dinners, and wedding receptions. According to Michael Albert, the former Facilities' Manager, in the 1990s, a couple rented the dining hall for their daughter's wedding reception. The mother of the bride came in the night before the reception to inspect it and objected to Sarah's portrait overseeing events. Dining hall staff attempted to dissuade her from removing the portrait, but the mother of the bride ordered that it be taken down, so the portrait was placed against a wall in the corner of the kitchen.

The next day, while the reception was in full swing, the wedding cake was brought out and placed on a table in front of the fireplace. The table and cake were directly beneath the wall where Sarah's portrait should have been. Suddenly, for no apparent reason, the table collapsed and the wedding cake went crashing to the floor.

In May of 2007, during the planning of another wedding reception, the bride objected to Sarah's portrait. The woman's somber visage did not match the decor she had selected. Staff cautioned her as best they could against removing the portrait. The bride ordered that if the portrait were not removed it had

**Dining Hall, Wilson College.**

to be covered, so a cloth was draped over the painting the night before.

The next day, in the middle of the wedding reception, a circuit breaker tripped and power was cut off to the dining hall and kitchen. There was no music and there would be no food without power to the ovens, coffee makers, and kitchen equipment, and without functioning dishwashers, there would be a tremendous mess. The electrician was called, a man who had worked at the college for twenty years. After two hours of

**Sarah Wilson's Portrait.**

searching, he still could not find the source of the power outage. The wedding reception was ruined. Hours after the last guest left, the electrician finally succeeded in tracing out the power lines and found the culprit, a circuit breaker located above the kitchen in the guts of what remained of Old Main. The electrician could determine no reason for the breaker to trip. The breaker had not tripped in all the years the electrician had worked at Wilson College—and it has not tripped since.

"I always had a problem with people who messed around with Sarah Wilson's portrait," Michael Albert said. "It's part of Wilson and her portrait deserves to be where it is."

Events suggest that Sarah Wilson concurs.

**Gymnasium, Wilson College.**

# More Stories...

There are many ghost stories told by the alumnae and students at Wilson College.

Screams heard in the early hours of fall mornings at least once every year radiate from a small classroom on the top floor of Warfield Hall, a Gothic Revival classroom building just up the drive from Riddle. The source of these screams has been investigated by campus security as far back as the 1970s, but remains a mystery. The scream was recorded by accident during a student radio broadcast from Warfield in 1974. The tape of this broadcast has since been lost.

Students are often struck by an unsettling sense of being watched while walking in "the tunnel," an underground passageway connecting several Wilson dormitories, recreational facilities, and classrooms. Some

**Underground walkway at Wilson College known as the Tunnel.**

have complained of suddenly inhaling a repulsive odor that appears and departs in one breath.

"It smells like rotting flesh," Albert explained, having experienced the mysterious phenomenon himself.

"There's no source for it. It's like walking through a wall, and then it's gone."

Students believe they have seen the ghost of a small child wandering through the third floor lobby of McElwain-Davison, a dormitory complex built on the footprint of Old Main, the original structure that housed Wilson students in the early years of the college.

The Wilson College gymnasium, built in 1877, is the site of unexplained footsteps and voices. The swimming pool beside it hosts phantom echoes.

And a malevolent shadow sometimes appears on the main campus, just out of range of vision. It is glimpsed in the corner of the eye and watches from the trees and shrubs. It has been known to follow and frighten, and even to touch unsuspecting students walking alone across the campus at night, toward the darkness of Riddle Hall.

**Warfield Hall, Wilson College.**

# The Antietam
# Humane Society

**8513 Lyons Road, Waynesboro, Pennsylvania**

Sometimes the dogs would bark at night. Ellen had worried about this at first, living across the street from the animal shelter, wondering if the dogs would bark at night and keep them up.

The small dogs would start first: faint, high-pitched yipping sounds. They would be joined moments later by the medium-sized dogs' louder, slightly fuller barks. Finally the large dogs would join in, their low, rumbling bellows fleshing out the choir.

She did not hear the dogs in the beginning. The barking did not start until later.

Florence Lyon was a well-known and well-respected affluent and slightly eccentric lifetime resident of Waynesboro. Her family fortune had come from dairy cows and thoroughbreds, and she lived in a sprawling farm that had occupied hundreds of acres along the East branch of the Antietam Creek. When Lyon passed away in 1973, her love of animals was reflected in the terms of her will. She had directed that fifty-four acres and $250,000 be utilized to create the Antietam Humane Society. A barn and trust funds to care for her twenty-two animals were included in the estate, as was a small house located directly across the road

**Antietam Humane Society.**

from the shelter. The house was designated for use by the shelter manager, but eventually became a rental property, generating income for the shelter.

That was how Ellen had come to be there. Her mother, Sarah, was the shelter's Assistant Director. It made sense to accept Sarah's invitation to live there with her in the rented house, Ellen, her husband, John, and their infant son, Carson. They would save money and, with her mother right there or just across the street during the day, childcare would not be an issue. Her husband agreed, and they all settled into the small, two-story house.

Carson slept in his crib in Ellen and John's bedroom. The bedroom next to theirs would be Carson's when he was older. Sarah set her bedroom up in the finished attic.

All had been well in the house and all had been quiet at night—until the time came for Carson to sleep in his own room.

That was when Ellen first began to notice that sometimes the dogs would bark at night—the same nights that Carson would wake up screaming.

Carson had never been any trouble at night and was normally a sound, heavy sleeper. When he was almost twelve months old, his parents moved his crib into the bedroom next to theirs.

The first night was brutal. Carson woke up sometime between midnight and 2 a.m., wailing. Ellen rushed to his crib and snatched him up. She could feel his body shivering. Solving the issue in the usual fashion, Carson slept in his parents' bed that night. Okay, his mother reasoned. This is normal. He'll get used to his room and settle in eventually.

But he didn't. Most nights, always between the hours of midnight and 2 a.m., Carson would wake up, apparently startled by something, and sob. Sometimes he would wake up and scream.

When he was old enough, they put him in a toddler bed. Carson would climb down from the bed at night and cry. Sometimes they would find him sleeping on the floor in the family room in the morning.

"We never had any inkling why this child would not sleep in there," Ellen recounted years later. "If we put him in our bed, he would sleep all night. If we put him on the couch, he would sleep all night. If we would put him anywhere, he would sleep, *except in that room*."

As time wore on, Ellen started to wake up every night in anticipation of the nightly disturbance. And it was on one such night, when she woke up first, that she *saw* the Lady.

"I was sound asleep. I woke up and she was there."

Ellen could see her son's bed from her open bedroom door and glanced in that direction, but on this night her view was obstructed... and Ellen saw instead a woman looking down at her from the side of her bed. "She had long, straight hair; it wasn't blonde hair, but it wasn't real dark, and she had on a long, light colored skirt and a long-sleeved light shirt." The skirt was very full and it appeared to her to resemble clothing worn in the mid-1800s. "I don't remember anything about her face, other than I was scared to death!"

Ellen jumped out of bed and the Lady vanished. "She was just gone," she said.

Her husband stirred and asked her what had happened. They both decided it had been a dream.

A week later she would find out she was pregnant with their second child.

**House owned by the Antietam Humane Society.**

Carson was seven years old when his brother David was born. Although he still refused to sleep in his room at night, it had become less of an issue since Carson typically found his way to the couch or went up to sleep in his grandmother's room without disturbing anyone.

As David approached his first birthday, Carson took part of the attic as his bedroom and David's crib was moved into Carson's room.

"David was sleeping through the night and was an excellent baby," Ellen recalled. "He slept through the night at a very early age. We never had an ounce of problem."

She and her husband decided they would not allow David to sleep in their bed or be freed from his room at night, as had been the case with Carson. Both believed now that Carson's inability to sleep in his room stemmed from their leniency in the beginning.

But the very first night David spent in what was now his room, he woke up bawling. And it happened the next night, and the next. Every night, between 12 and 2 a.m., David woke up and cried.

*What* was going on?

And then one night she saw her again—the Lady—only this time the apparition was leaning over David's crib. "What are you doing?" Ellen yelled as she flew from her bed to David's crib, scaring her husband and waking Carson and Sarah upstairs. But the Lady had long disappeared, just as she had the first time, and just as she would again and again in the weeks and months that followed as Ellen raced toward her in the night to get her away from her son.

# The Lady

### "Everyone thought I was losing my mind."

Ellen's mother believed her, but her husband didn't and Carson never told them why he would not sleep in that room. She had no idea what to do. But then the day came when she knew she had to do *something*.

David was down for his nap in his crib and Ellen thought she would run across the street to the shelter for just a moment to see her mother. She had never left either of her sons while they napped, but David was sound asleep and it would only be across the street where she could see the house at all times and it would only be for a second. She had called ahead of time, and Sarah met her outside, at

**Front door of the house owned by the Antietam Humane Society.**

the front door. As Ellen said hello to her mother, something suddenly told her to turn around.

She looked back across the street to her house.

The Lady was standing in the doorway.

She screamed, "She's standing in the door! Don't you see her?"

But Sarah saw nothing as Ellen flew across the street to the house and through the front door...to where she *saw* the Lady standing—the doorway to her son's bedroom where he lay sound asleep—but no one was there.

It was Sarah who finally decided that they had to do something.

Sarah had worked at the Humane Society almost since its inception and had worked her way up to Assistant Director. Over the years she had earned extra income by taking care of patrons' pets while they vacationed or were away for one reason or another. She had regular clients whose animals she fed every day before she came to work and others she cared for at night. She walked dogs, fed cats, and even took care of a few goats and horses.

There was a woman who lived in Cascade, Maryland, just across the Pennsylvania line, whose dogs she had walked and whose cats she had fed. Her name was Deborah. She loved animals and was a consistent and loyal patron of the Humane Society. She also happened to be a psychic.

## *The Reluctant Psychic*

Deborah had come to unwanted national attention when, more than ten years before, she had read an article in a morning paper about a police department whose dog had disappeared during training in a forested area of Maryland. "I know where your dog is," she told the officer in charge of the K-9 Unit, convinced he would dismiss her as a lunatic and hang up on her. He did not. Deborah found their dog.

She went on to work on more than fifty homicides and missing persons cases for various local, state, and federal law enforcement organizations (although the federal agencies would never admit it), until she grew weary of the attitudes and the constant "testing" of her abilities by skeptical officers and withdrew to a quieter life in the Blue Ridge Summit area of Franklin County. She was known for her work at the Blue Ridge Summit Free Library, loved by the children for the story hour she hosted every Saturday, and known by the residents as the person to seek out when your pet goes missing.

But every now and then Deborah would get a telephone call like the one she had received from Sarah.

Sarah was on one extension and Ellen was on the other. They described what had gone on with Carson and what was occurring now with David, but before Ellen mentioned what she had seen, Deborah interrupted. "There's a woman there."

Deborah described the Lady's appearance all the way down to the type of shoes she wore. "She's just looking over the baby to make sure he's okay," she assured them. "That's where she took care of her own children."

She went on to explain that the entity was not malevolent; she was just doing what she always had. "You need to tell her to go into the light," Deborah instructed. "Tell her that everything is all right, the children are safe, and she doesn't need to check on them and that she should go into the light."

It seemed far-fetched, like something out of a low-grade television movie. But Sarah agreed to do it.

"So I hung up the phone, sat on the floor of David's bedroom, and began to speak to the Lady."

As Ellen watched, Sarah spoke out loud to whatever had been bothering the children. Sarah reassured her that the children were safe and that she was free now and to go into the light. She did this three times.

Sarah had just finished the third repetition when something grabbed her from inside—a cold, bitter metallic freeze twisted its way through her body in a swirling mass of crystalline breath. She shivered violently.

"It was like this rush," Sarah recounted. "I can't really explain it. Cold, bitter, bitter cold. It just went through me. It was just weird. I never felt anything like that before."

And then...*it* was gone.

~~~~~~~

The nights settled into a peaceful, uninterrupted rhythm. David slept in his room without incident, the Lady never reappeared, and Ellen's family went on with the simple business of living. Eventually they moved on to a larger house.

Carson, now a young man, never explained or spoke to anyone about what had startled him awake every night. "It was so long ago, I just couldn't tell you," he claimed to those who pursued this story.

But after much prodding, persuaded by adulthood and distance, Carson stated, "It just felt like something was always looking at me. Weird. I never saw anything, but I always felt there was something around me. There was someone always there…but they weren't."

# Epilogue

Another family now lives in the house across from the Antietam Humane Society—a young couple and their three-year-old son. He was recently moved into his own room.

His mother and Ellen are acquainted, and in a recent conversation, she lamented that her son would not sleep in his room. "He will not sleep in that room," she said. "He won't even play in his room anymore. He takes all his toys out and plays in the family room."

Ellen wavered between telling her everything and telling her nothing. "Why won't he sleep there?" she gingerly asked.

Her friend looked at her, sighed, and said, "He told me there are monsters there."

# 3

# The Beauty Parlor

It has been said that hairdressers and beauticians are the keepers of the world's greatest secrets. Most women go to the same shop and to the same hairdresser for years, particularly when the establishment is a small, personal neighborhood salon. While their hair is being washed, dyed, highlighted, curled, or cut, women, relaxing in the pampered atmosphere, tend to speak openly of their lives and passions to the safe, familiar "friend" tending their tresses. This emotional energy saturates the atmosphere, humming just below the sounds of voices, hair dryers, and running water.

One such place sits on the side of a hill, in the basement of an aged building in a small town in Franklin County. It is a small, quaint shop consisting of one large room divided into areas for washing, cutting, and waiting. On the wall next to the counter is a large bulletin board, and pinned in rows in one corner of the bulletin board are photographs of patrons who have died.

The owners, Betty and Martha, have been in business for more than forty years and have been at their current location for more than two decades. In parallel lives they have shared their clients' marriages, births, and deaths, bound by stories told through countless haircuts and hundreds of hours of personal care. However, over the past several years, strange episodes have invaded their routines. Both no longer feel comfortable in the shop at night when the lights are turned off just before closing. They have sensed a lingering presence in the dark, staying behind, refusing to leave. They have witnessed and experienced unexplained events, but only Betty will speak of the things she has seen.

# Ghostly Occurrences

### *The Mist*

One day, one of Betty's clients began to cry as she sat under the hair dryer. It happened just after the delivery man came and went, someone who had been servicing the shop for years and someone whom the client had seen many times before.

Betty brought her some tissues and asked her what was wrong. The tearful woman replied that she had "recognized her husband in the delivery man," and her longing for her husband, who had died years before, had saddened her to the point of tears.

Betty escorted her client from the dryer and sat her in the chair where Betty would style her hair. The woman sat facing the mirror and Betty stood behind her. As Betty began removing the curlers from her customer's hair, both were startled by something emanating from the woman's lap.

"It was like a white, heavy fog," Betty recalled. The cloud suddenly appeared in front of her client as if it had risen up out of her. "It happened very quickly, but it came out of this woman's lap; circled and floated up above her head." Betty felt nothing as she watched the vapor pass through her hands. As the mist rose above their heads it disintegrated, disappearing as mysteriously as it had appeared.

Betty had never before seen or experienced anything like that. She quickly glanced about the shop to see if anyone else had noticed the mist. While other people were there, including Martha, the co-owner of the shop, none of them had noticed anything unusual.

Betty's startled customer looked up at her, leaned back, and asked, "What was that?"

"I said I didn't know," Betty recounted. Neither woman knew what to make of the mist. Later they would conclude it had been caused by the woman's profound sadness. "This woman has been my customer for twenty-five years," Betty went on. "She told me that she has had 'things' happen to her in her house." Betty shrugged. "So I think [whatever it is], it's with the customer. She brought it here."

But Betty isn't sure.

## Mirrors, Signs, and Smudges

It was a Friday evening and Betty was in the shop with a lone customer when the mirror on the wall beside them appeared to levitate outward from the wall and just hang suspended in the air—as if an unseen hand held the mirror straight out, away from the wall. Moments later, the mirror set itself back securely on its hook.

Betty had seen the mirror swing on occasion, but had dismissed it as being the result of vibrations from movement in the shop. This, however, was different. The mirror had clearly *projected itself* outward from the wall.

On another evening, again while Betty was the only stylist in the shop with a customer, both watched as a sign on the wall near the counter lifted itself up and jumped off the wall. "The sign basically came off the wall and threw itself on the floor," Betty recounted. The placard had been on the wall next to the bulletin board bearing the photographs of deceased customers. A telephone sat on the counter, and, looking to see where the sign had fallen, both saw that the telephone's cord was swinging.

"What in the world would make it do that?" Betty exclaimed, to which her customer matter-of-factly replied, "I believe you have a ghost."

Betty laughed this off and proceeded to tend to her client's hair. After a while, her client said, "Betty, I hate to tell you, but it's here."

"What do you mean?" Betty asked, and her client replied with a chill in her voice, "*It's* right here. *It's* large. I *feel* it. *It's* standing here, right between the stations."

Betty looked up and saw something transparent but refractive occupying the space in front of them. Looking through it, everything on the other side appeared distorted. Betty was not able to read the labels on the bottles of hair products she kept at her station and reflections in the mirror were smudged. "It was like looking with bad eyesight," Betty explained. "It was clear but blurry."

The distorted mass remained for a few moments more...and then dissipated.

# Epilogue

Betty and Martha still run their beauty parlor up on the hill, providing friendly, professional service to their many loyal customers. The days and evenings essentially pass in comfortable, uneventful routine, with people coming and going, talking and laughing, enjoying the company and attention. A new client appears now and then to take the place of one whose picture appears on the bulletin board, the salon's memorial to clients who have passed on.

Sometimes the mirror swings on its hook and sometimes a mysterious gossamer curtain comes between Betty and her workstation, distorting her view, but disappearing as quickly as it descends. She has gotten used to it.

But no one ever stays there alone at night.

*Author's note:*
*The location of the shop and identities of the participants*
*aren't given to protect their privacy.*

# 4

# The Old Jail

**175 East King Street, Chambersburg, Pennsylvania**

## The Dungeon

### *The Love Story...*

She was beautiful. He did not care that she was older. She had confided to him the most intimate details of her unhappy life and he did not care what other people would think. She was the only one for him and he was the only one for her.

He was barely twenty and she was almost thirty, but he did not think about the age difference or about her status, how she was so far above him that he never thought she'd so much as acknowledge his presence, much less seek it out. She was well known in the community, both for her beauty and for the fact that she was the wife of the man who owned, along with his partner, the most popular hostelry in Chambersburg. He, on the other hand, wasn't known at all; save for the people whose drinks he filled every night at the tavern.

With the westward expansion of the population and the construction of turnpikes across the states of Pennsylvania and Maryland in the early 1800s, Chambersburg became a transportation and commercial hub. By the time the Cumberland Valley Railroad reached Chambersburg in 1837, the streets were filled with shops catering to the travelers and businessmen frequenting the area.

**Old Jail, Chambersburg.**

Taverns combined with hostels, known as hostelries, dotted the area.

That was where he had first met her, at the tavern attached to the hotel, when she had come in one night on the arm of her husband. Her husband seemed to know everyone and sang out greetings to the crowd. When her husband left her at the counter to speak to a group of men at a nearby table, their eyes met. She leaned toward him and whispered, "Help me!"

And that was when, along with everything else he did not think about, he stopped thinking about the fact that she was his employer's wife.

They began to meet in secret, at locations where he believed they would not be recognized. Longing for one another, their precautions vanished when she came to him in his room one night. She wept in his arms. She told him that her husband abused her. He was possessive and unyielding, resentful of the looks and attention bestowed upon her by other men. When angered by some perceived infraction, her husband would beat her.

She cried that she had had no one to go to as no one in town would ever believe her. But she had known, from their first gaze, that she could trust him. Only him.

They began to plan their departure. He saved his money and hid his contempt for his employer. Although they continued to consummate their affair in his room on nights her husband was away, it never occurred to him that they would be discovered.

The wife of her husband's partner would prove to be the agent of their downfall. She had come to suspect something was amiss when she noticed the glances between the lowly tavern attendant and the Mistress. Under different circumstances, this would be of no interest to her, as she knew that many women were unsatisfied with their lot and, although illegal, dalliances occurred among all classes, including shop owners and hosteliers. This, however, was different. It was very dangerous because the actions of the Mistress affected her own self-interests. She had extravagant tastes and the money her husband gave her from his lucrative partnership in the hostelry fed her endless needs. The economic toll of a scandal involving any of them would be devastating and she would likely lose her open-ended purchasing power. She could never allow this to happen.

She followed the Mistress to the young man's boarding house one night and saw the tavern worker when he greeted her.

No one knows for certain how his Mistress found out that they had been discovered. What is known is that she somehow managed to escape to somewhere just outside of Philadelphia. It's likely she used the money he had been saving for them to pay for the train that took her there.

The young man, however, was not as fortunate. He was dragged from his room at night by her husband's partner and taken to the jail on King Street.

### It's Tragic Ending...

They are in the dungeon in the basement, to the right of the stairs, adjacent to the room where the guards sit, socialize, and drink. It is sometime during the first half of the nineteenth century, years before the Civil War. The cell hosts two sets of manacles that hang from the wall from huge bolts. Prisoners are typically secured there while they are "questioned." But they are not being used tonight. The prisoner thrown down the stairs and pulled into the dungeon has begun this night still on his feet. He is cowering in the far corner.

Although he is not a guard and has no authority in the jail, the partner of the wronged husband is directing the two guards

**Basement rooms, Old Jail.**

accompanying him. He has fine, brownish hair flecked with gold and a thick, flat mustache. He is wearing grey slacks, a white shirt that is open at the collar and a short vest. The vest and pants are made of wool and there are tiny light stripes in the grey material. He looks like he came home from church, took off his coat, and came down to the jail to beat someone. He is livid that word is going to come out that his friend's wife had an affair and that she somehow managed to get away from them. The only individual left upon whom they can vent their wrath is the poor young man they have thrown into the dungeon.

He raises a heavy wooden plank he has obtained from the guards and smashes it across the prisoner's back. Blood splatters from the wound and the stricken man's mouth.

The guards are not wearing uniforms; they appear to be in street clothes, but they are clearly employees of the jail. They, too, pounce on the man, now screaming in pain, and beat him to the ground, one wielding a chain and the other striking with a metal pipe.

The young man begs for his life. "But I loved her," he pleads between cries for mercy.

The man in the suit curses him and the three men hit him over and

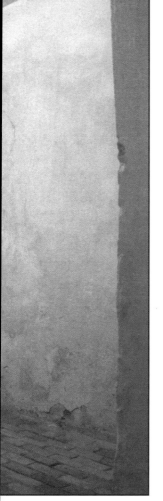

over with the plank, the chain, and the pipe until blood has coated the walls and splattered onto their hands, clothes, and faces. By the time the poor man dies it seems as if there is more blood outside of his body than within.

No one would remember his name and no one would notice his passing. His blood would remain in the porous surfaces of the stone walls and floor for decades along with the blood from scores of other unfortunates who were taken to the dungeon to the right of the stairs. Although the floor has been paved over, bloodstains remain in the bricks underneath.

His Mistress would never return, disappearing into a new life with a new name in a city hundreds of miles away. She had not been there then to hear his cries. She is not there today.

But her young lover, abandoned and left to face the rage of his murderers, might still linger, trapped by the turmoil of his intense love and horrible death. Workers at the Old Jail have heard moaning and other sounds coming from the basement and visitors have often complained of chills and cold spots upon touring the dungeons and holding cells below. And even though the stone walls are three feet thick and the window has been covered over, passersby on the sidewalk on West King Street have heard faint cries coming from somewhere inside the Old Jail at night.

**Dungeon, Old Jail.**

Above-ground addition, circa 1880, Old Jail.

# The Old Jail Today

Franklin County's "Old Jail" was erected in 1818 and remained in continuous operation until 1970, longer than any other jail in Pennsylvania. Constructed with three-foot thick stone and brick walls, eight solitary cells, basement dungeons, and a gallows, the jail was feared and known for its conditions and outcomes. The jail survived the burning of Chambersburg by Confederate soldiers during the Civil War in 1864 and was expanded and modernized in 1880. The last man to be hanged in Franklin County met his fate on the gallows in the jail yard in 1912 (see Mont Alto story). The jail was saved from demolition in the early 1970s and today, in addition to being the home for the Franklin County Historical Society–Kittochtinny, operates as a museum and library offering numerous services to visitors.

The lives that have passed through the dungeons and cells have left residual imprints on the stone walls and brick floors and in the atmosphere where the air is always still but full. The cells on the first floor of the jail and those added in 1880 do not project the same mood as do the rooms and tunnels in the basement. Inmates held here did not, for the most part, seem to experience the dread prevalent in the air downstairs.

## *The Apparitions*

The room to the right of the stairs as one descends into the basement of the jail appears to have been used as a break or meeting room for the guards. In stark contrast to the energy present in other areas of the basement, whoever regularly occupied this room was not in fear of anything. Men smoked, drank, and ate there, sitting on stools around a small table playing cards while others played a board game involving a piece of wood about a foot long and four inches wide. The wood bore small holes into which white pegs were placed and moved. Some occupants sat on chairs, leaning back against the walls on two legs, watching the card and board games. The people in this room were in control, and were not afraid of anything.

It's been reported that the walls of the two solitary dungeons to the left of the staircase are drenched in fear. Hopelessness permeates the stale air. People held here were alone, stripped of all contact with the outside world and whatever lives they had led. They were left here to await their fate. A prisoner would sit there alone with no one to comfort him, no one to confide in, or protest to. Knowing that this was it, there was no turning back... no escape from this room. Even if an inmate managed to break free and run, he would be killed anyway. Whoever was shackled here knew they were going to die and knew death would not be gentle.

The energy from one of these unfortunate souls remains in one of these cells. He might be of African descent. He is shackled and sits cross-legged on the floor. He is going to be executed and laments that he is not ready to meet his Maker. He claims he did not commit the crime for which he has been convicted. While three men were executed on the gallows after the Old Jail was constructed, some of the condemned were held there in transit to other jails where they would meet their fate. He might be one of these. Or he might be someone executed by other means after hanging was banned in the Commonwealth of Pennsylvania in 1913.

The adjacent hallways and tunnels bear the same tension: a combination of fear, resignation, and anger. As one descends deeper into the heart of the basement, the feeling of a hand brushing the back of one's neck or the glimpse of a shadow darting away is not uncommon.

The hallway bearing the most tension leads to the two cells that served as waiting areas for the gallows. Steps inside lead up to an outside door that opens into the jail yard, a grassy expanse surrounded by three-foot thick, twenty-foot high limestone walls. The gallows dominates the center of the green.

Overwhelmed by the knowledge of what was going to happen to them, it was not uncommon for the condemned to collapse in the hallway and have to be dragged into the holding cells by the arms.

**Guard area in the basement of the Old Jail.**

[61]

Isolation cell in the basement of the Old Jail.

**Hallway by the gallows cells in the basement of the Old Jail.**

# The Gallows

From the arrival of the first colonists in the 1600s and up until 1913, execution by hanging was the preferred method of capitol punishment in the Commonwealth of Pennsylvania. These executions were public spectacles and attracted huge crowds of onlookers. In 1834, Pennsylvania became the first state in the Union to abolish public hangings. This left the responsibility for carrying out executions to each individual county. The result was that a limited number of passes or tickets were provided to the public for viewing "private hangings." Nothing could be done, however, to prevent people from watching from rooftops and other structures outside of the jail yard. Add to this the generally inflammatory press coverage, and the result was that hangings essentially remained much-anticipated public events.

At least four executions in Franklin County were carried out prior to the construction of the Old Jail. The executions took place on land east of the existing Chambersburg Post Office on Lincoln Way East, in an area that became known as "Gallows Hill." Three of the condemned men were convicted of murder and one was convicted of rape.

Three hangings have taken place in the jail yard at the Old Jail.

> ➤ Hezekiah Shaffer was convicted of murdering his wife and was scheduled for execution Thursday, April 17, 1879. However, on Monday, April 14, he somehow obtained a knife and cut his arms and legs in a suicide attempt. He survived, but was extremely weak from loss of blood. His execution was rescheduled for April 19.
> On the morning of the execution, crowds began to gather around the jail by 9 a.m. Shaffer was too weak to walk or stand so he was wrapped in a blanket and carried to the gallows by six men. He was seated in a chair on top of the drop door and the rope was placed around his neck. When the door sprang open, the chair fell away and the execution was completed.
>
> ➤ Peter "Peachy" Swingler, convicted of killing another man in an argument over a woman, was executed June 5, 1879.
>
> ➤ The last person executed on the gallows in the jail yard was William Reed. Convicted for the murder of Sarah Matheny of Mont Alto, Reed was hanged April 30, 1912. *(See Mont Alto story.)*

The gallows used for Shaffer and Swingler had been stored in a vault under the courthouse steps. Several weeks before Reed's scheduled execution, it was discovered that something was seriously wrong with the gallows. Shaffer and Swingler had strangled to death, unnecessarily prolonging their suffering. This occurred because the drop was a single door, went down slowly, and the cross beam was not high enough to give a long, full drop to the body. Therefore, the drop was neither fast nor strong enough to snap their necks and they endured an agonizing death by suffocation.

**The gallows.**

Franklin County requested and was granted use of the gallows from Berks County. The gallows was transported to Chambersburg via the Western Maryland Railroad and wheeled through the streets of the town to the Old Jail several days before Reed's scheduled execution.

When hanging ceased to be used as a method for execution in Pennsylvania, the gallows was loaned out to the state of Maryland. Eventually it was returned to Franklin County where it rests today, in the jail yard of the Old Jail.

No readily available records indicate how many souls met their fate on the trap doors of the gallows at the Old Jail. The energy surrounding this instrument of death is so pervasive that few can look upon it without reaction. The sounds of the crowds who witnessed the executions sometimes echoes faintly through the yard late at night, disturbing the quiet but never noticed by the passing cars on West King Street or Second Street. Sometimes the latches on the double drop doors creak when workers stroll through the jail yard. Sometimes the gallows appears to shudder, as if an unseen weight has suddenly shifted. The faithful old gallows almost seems to know it will never be used again. Currently awaiting demolition, an exact replica is scheduled to be constructed in its place.

Whatever may or may not be lingering from decades past, the majority of visitors to the Old Jail will never sense or see anything out of the ordinary. Some might experience slight, unidentifiable discomfort and will dismiss the sensation as "nothing." Others might feel nervous or anxious and not know why. Still others might not be able to catch their breath in places or feel a deep dread in their chest. But those more sensitive to energies and impressions might feel the presence of sorrowful entities being beaten and dragged through hallways and doors, crying out in anguish at their fate, voices muffled by the passage of time and the metallic clatter of dragging chains.

# 5

# The Chambersburg Heritage Center

## 100 Lincoln Way East, Chambersburg, Pennsylvania

**Entrance to the Chambersburg Heritage Center.**

S he had been working at the Chambersburg Heritage Center for several months before the first incident occurred. She didn't really think much about it when it first happened. She had come in early, as she always did, around 7 a.m. As the Center's receptionist, she was always the first one there. She would turn on the lights and the computers and prepare the space for the public. Others would follow a half hour to an hour later.

There had been nothing unusual about that particular morning. No storms had swept through the area the night before and there certainly hadn't been any earthquakes. Yet nearly a dozen books had somehow freed themselves from the bookcase and were lying scattered on the floor.

The Chambersburg Heritage Center occupies a recently renovated marble building located on the east corner of the diamond in downtown Chambersburg, across the street from the Franklin County Courthouse on Lincoln Way East. As with all structures in Chambersburg, the location has witnessed centuries of change. The Valley National Bank occupied the site for more than one hundred years, first in a wooden structure and then in the existing marble building that was completed in 1915. The non-profit Heritage Center opened for business in the former bank building on July 16, 2004.

The main hall hosts educational displays and exhibitions, with the two-story building having facilities for conferences and research. The gift shop offers souvenirs and educational items based on the history of Chambersburg and Franklin County. Numerous books by historians and local authors are displayed on shelves and in bookcases.

Sometimes visitors will disturb the displays and a book or trinket might accidentally fall, but she had never seen anything like this before. This

**The Chambersburg Heritage Center.**

had never happened. Books had never fallen out of the bookcases en masse and nothing had ever fallen from the shelves, at least not at night, when no one was there.

She wondered, could the cleaning people have done this? No, they were very conscientious and had never left anything amiss. Could a large truck rumbling by on the busy street outside have generated enough of a vibration to jar the books loose? Perhaps. But then, why hadn't *all* of them tumbled out? And why hadn't this happened before, or during the day? It wasn't as if trucks passed by on that busy stretch of the Lincoln Highway only at night.

**The gift shop at the Chambersburg Heritage Center.**

She had unlocked the main door, come in, and walked over to the reception desk where she would spend her day when she saw the books on the floor. Walking over to them, she glanced about to see if anything else had been disturbed, but it appeared as if all the other items in the gift shop were in their proper place. She looked at the bookcase from where the books had fallen. Neighboring books still sat firmly in line, now sporting gaps where the fallen volumes had been. The eight books had dislodged themselves from between other books and from three different shelves.

It wasn't until she picked up the books and returned the errant volumes to their original locations that she noticed they were all by the same author. Then she thought for a moment and checked to see if the eight books on the floor were all they had by this particular author. They were. She wasn't exactly startled, but this observation did give her pause. How strange, she thought. What a coincidence that all of the books by this one author would fall out of the bookcase at night, from three different shelves, while all the other books remained untouched.

The books were a series of historical romance novels set during the Civil War and had been written by a Chambersburg resident.

She had almost forgotten about it when it happened again. The same books scattered on the floor in front of the bookcase, taken from different shelves while no other books had been disturbed.

So, without telling anyone, she rearranged the bookcase and moved all of the books in question to different locations. This lasted a few weeks. She came in one morning and the now familiar books greeted her from the floor. Nothing else had been disturbed.

Two more times she moved the books and two more times they made their way onto the floor, always the same books by the

**Bookcase in the Chambersburg Heritage Center Gift Shop.**

same author—*all of them*—and never any other books by any other author. Over the weeks the gift shop had sold some of the novels and had received additional replacement copies, but no matter what the count, these books—and *just* these books—would end up on the floor.

Weeks and months have passed since that first morning she found the books on the floor. The gift shop has been re-arranged a few times and the books have been removed from the bookcase and now rest on shelves along the wall. And while they haven't yet fallen from their new locations, volunteers and staff members alike have come to expect that some day they will. For even though no one will come right out and admit it, the books, from time to time, appear to move.

# The Farmer's Wife

**103 South Carlisle Street,
Greencastle, Pennsylvania**

## Home Away from Home

### "This is where you belong."

Marilyn Newcomer always had a love for antiques. "When I was young, I collected old books," she said. But it wasn't until she retired that she was able to devote the time and attention she needed to fully pursue her passion. She began to go to auctions and accumulated many valuable and unique items. It was her daughter who suggested she look into renting space in antique shops to sell some of the treasures she had accumulated.

Marilyn thrived on the buying and selling cycle of the business. She rented booths in various locations and became well known in the local area for the quality of antiques she offered. Some time in 2003, people she had met at an auction approached her about setting up space in an antique shop they planned to open in Greencastle. A friend encouraged her to go see it.

The building at 103 South Carlisle Street dates from the first decade of the 1900s. A staircase along the south side of the

**The Farmer's Wife, Greencastle.**

building connects the two attics and basement to the main floor. The former headquarters for L. H. Leiter Hardware was used for various stores and shops as it changed hands over the next one hundred years until it eventually became home to antique dealers on the main floor and a fitness center in the basement.

Marilyn walked into the store and within a few feet of the entrance, she was overwhelmed by a sense of belonging, almost a feeling of being at home. The building told her, "You're supposed to be here, Marilyn. This is where you belong." It just felt right.

A short time later, the owners decided to sell and she was able to purchase the building. "It wasn't planned," she said. "It just happened."

## "Stuff started happening."

Marilyn's family helped her get the shop organized. One night just after she acquired the property, Marilyn, some family members, and friends took a break from their work to go to dinner. Before they left, Marilyn made certain all the lights were off and the doors were locked.

An hour later, they returned to find every light on and every door still locked.

Each night, prior to closing, Marilyn would make no less than three trips around the store, ensuring that all lights were off and all doors locked. Each morning when she opened, lights were on, sometimes all of them.

Then the bells started. Customers and employees heard the tinkling of bells coming from somewhere inside the store. A sound made by bells that were not there.

The bells followed no pattern. Sometimes the sound was loud and startling, as if the bells were close by. Other times the sound was faint, but distinctive.

Small items such as keys or cell phones seemed to move to the edges of counters or fall onto the floor. The cordless phone was frequently out of its cradle.

Customers and workers often heard footsteps in the attic; heavy, deliberate footsteps, and everyone who spent time there began to feel as though they were being followed.

Marilyn's granddaughter was working in the store alone one Saturday night. She called, frightened. "I wish it would just go away," she told Marilyn. "It's following me everywhere."

"I told her I knew exactly what she was talking about." Marilyn suggested she turn on the television as a distraction. Marilyn remained on the telephone with her until her father came to take her home.

The front door was heard opening and then closing, but no customers appeared in the store. This happened to Marilyn one day while her back was to the front of the store and she was working at the computer. She looked up expecting to see a customer, but no one was there. Turning back to her computer, she began to get the feeling someone *was* there...right next to her. She decided to try a different approach and said, "Okay, Mr. Ghostie. We're buddies. I'm not going to be afraid of you anymore. Hang out as long as you want."

Immediately after uttering this friendly compromise, she felt a dark, cold breath in her ear as garbled sounds ordered her to get out.

She did.

**Inside the Farmer's Wife, showing a wide variety of collectibles and antiques.**

# Ghostly Occurrences

## *Shadows in the Basement*

The basement of the building at 103 South Carlisle Street has housed for a number of years a popular fitness center for women. Fitness equipment is set up in various stations around the facility.

One of the employees typically comes in early to open. One particular day, a few ladies came in with her and went to the back area to begin their workout. Moments later, they called to her to come look. She went back to where they pointed. On the floor, in front of one of the pieces of equipment, was a circle of small stones about the size of large pebbles. The stones had no logical source as there were none in the facility and the building sat on a paved lot.

Sometimes the equipment appears to move. Just by inches, here and there.

And another employee often finds lights turned off at night by one employee on in the morning.

Items on the front sign-in counter are moved and paperwork will drift in a non-existent breeze across the counter to the floor.

A filing cabinet and several pieces of equipment are located toward the back of the room at the base of the stairway connecting the basement to the antique shop above. The paperwork in this filing cabinet is frequently disturbed. At least once a week a worker straightens it out. The drawers and files are attacked at night and found scattered in the morning.

Many patrons have complained of an odd, musty odor that comes and goes. The basement has been checked for mold and other possible sources, but none has been found. Some have described the smell as that of a "wet dog."

Everyone has heard the bells: a tinkling kind of bell toward the back area by the stairway. Employees and clients, who have come in with their children, say their little ones are frightened by the bells and by something in the back. Children have even claimed they were being followed or watched.

And many who frequent the facility, during the day and at night, have seen a low, dark shadow *move* across the front of the stairway.

## *Apparitions*

Ghost hunters and those claiming sensitivity to unseen presences have visited The Farmer's Wife and have suggested that various entities move about the building, causing everything from the footsteps to the malfunctioning lights to the sounds of the tinkling bells.

Among these "unseen" visitors are two young children, a boy and a girl, who come and go from the main floor of the antique shop. They lived down the street during the early years of the building and appear to be seven to nine years old. While they don't appear to be poor, apparently they did not get enough to eat at home and would come to the shop where they were given treats or food. They were happy when they were there. They play and run around the main floor.

The attic is divided into two floors. The highest level at one time held horse collars with bells, harnesses, and leather items used on farms. The main attic was a work area where men crafted the items stored and sold in the shop. The spirit of one of these men is still there.

**Entrance to the fitness facility located to the rear of The Farmer's Wife antique shop.**

He is someone who worked with his hands. From his clothing and the history of the building, it is likely he was a leather worker. He is wearing a blue, almost denim-like open-necked shirt and has a scarf of some sort tied around his neck. His pants are baggy at the top and get tighter around the ankles. Over his clothes he is wearing what appears to be a leather work vest or apron.

His dog is with him. It appears to be a large, grayish-black, longhaired dog. It is wolf-like in appearance, except for its ears, which hang down. It is shaggy and dirty from being out in the woods. The craftsman clearly loves his dog and he takes it with him everywhere.

Believed to be in his 30s and handsome, John loved his work. He was very happy there and believes it is where he belongs. He walks the building with his dog because it is *his* building and *he* is responsible for it. He is looking out for his building and for everyone who comes there.

It is suggested that it's John who plays pranks on the current employees and patrons of the antique shop and the health club in the basement, and that it is he who follows and watches, accompanied by the low, dark shadow cast by his beloved dog.

# Epilogue

Today *footsteps* can still be heard around the attic. *Something* still follows the customers and the workers, and the lights go off and on at will. Musty smells still emanate from an unknown source down in the fitness center and the filing cabinet continues to disrupt itself. A fleeting shadow is sometimes seen scurrying by the staircase.

But the most consistent phenomenon remains the ringing of non-extant bells. The sound of ringing bells is so common that Marilyn mentions them in her antique shop ads.

# The House
# in Blue Ridge Summit

T he door had moved.

He had been working on the closet door on the third floor of the old farmhouse when he heard footsteps downstairs at the main entrance, two floors below. He hadn't heard anyone come in, but someone was definitely wandering around down there.

The eighteenth century farmhouse was built into the side of a steep grade in the forested hills of Blue Ridge Summit, in the southeastern corner of Franklin County. The main door was at ground level in the front of the house, the second floor was accessible by a stairway and porch, and the third floor sat atop them where an attic should have been.

Faint but deliberate, the crisp tap of the distant footsteps sounded as if the visitor was wearing riding boots.

The newest owner of the farm had been a high-ranking law enforcement official in a high-profile government agency and had become familiar with Franklin County through friends and acquaintances from work. After visiting and investigating what the area had to offer, he and his wife agreed to move there when he retired.

"Hello?" he called.

He had not been expecting anyone. Although his wife usually spent time at the farmhouse working on projects, he was not expecting her as she was occupied at the large home they had previously purchased a few miles away. This second property was to be his "hobby" where he could build a woodworking shop and the farmhouse would serve as a guesthouse.

His wife had found this little farm shortly after they purchased the big house. She had been drawn to the farmstead's isolated and peaceful setting. Although the previous owners had done a tremendous amount of restoration work on the formerly neglected farmhouse and grounds, some projects remained. An outbuilding had all but collapsed, the springhouse was covered with vines, and the gravel drive that led from the road to the house to the stone foundation of a long lost barn was so overgrown with grass and weeds that it required mowing. The rectangular stone that was a scar of a hotel that had burned down decades ago remained visible in the grass next to the house. Overgrown woods encroached from all directions, attempting to consume what remained of the cleared land. Broken branches reached down from neglected trees. Surrounded by a collapsing stonewall torn apart by weather and brush, headstones in the cemetery, identifying the remains of the original residents, crumbled at the edge of the yard.

He had always wanted a farmstead and dreamed of raising long-horned steers. The farm acreage certainly wasn't large enough to raise anything other than a few horses and maybe a goat or two, but his wife had fallen in love with the old stone house and the stone foundation at the end of the drive would serve as the base for his woodshop.

"Hello?" he called again.

In the ensuing months, he and his wife spent every free moment they had working on the house, sheds, and grounds, gingerly restoring the structures and clearing the property. He eventually built the workshop of his dreams and relished the isolation of the countryside. But the house—the *house* his wife had adored on first sight—bothered him. It had begun to bother him almost immediately, just after they prepared the rooms for their belongings.

The closet door in the small bedroom on the third floor needed to be repaired and he had removed the door from its hinges to work on the hardware. He set it against the closet and turned his attention downstairs.

The footsteps had stopped with his second hello.

He walked down the narrow, twisting staircase that connected all the floors and marveled at how physically small and agile people must have been when the house was built. He reached the first floor and was greeted with silence.

The door was shut and the lights were off.

This hadn't been the first time. He had lost count, actually, as to how many times he had heard footsteps or creaks or doors opening and closing and hoped that some day he would get used to the phenomena and wouldn't go to look.

And he hoped some day as well that he would be able to ignore the baffling isolated areas of frigid air he encountered now and then that made the hair on the back of his neck stand up and made him want to run out of the house.

But he knew he would never be able to figure out what it was exactly that bothered him on the third floor, especially in the hallway between the two bedroom doors.

He turned and headed back up the stairs. When he reached the second floor, he heard a loud thud come from the bedroom where he had been working on the closet door. He continued on up and went to the back bedroom to investigate and resume his project. Bitter cold surrounded him as the warmth drained from his body. He stared at the closet and at the door that had moved.

He had been in shoot-outs and hostage situations. He had been in charge of every crisis situation imaginable. He trusted his ability to deal with anything, anywhere, anytime. But *not* this... *not* these things he felt, but could *not* explain...things he heard, but could not see...and certainly *not* closet doors that slid along floors by themselves.

He left.

It would be weeks before he went back and finished.

# Blue Ridge Summit

When the Western Maryland Railroad reached the area in 1872, Blue Ridge Summit was transformed from a quiet, mountain retreat into a bustling vacation community for Baltimore and Washington, D.C. residents hoping to escape the heat of the city. Mammoth hotels sprang up along the hilltops and shops and services catering to the summer population brought prosperity.

Wallis Simpson, wife of Prince Edward, Duke of Windsor, was born there, and the Monterey Country Club is home to one of the oldest golf courses in the United States.

Blue Ridge Summit continued to thrive until the Great Depression of 1929, when money among the wealthy grew scarce. By the end of World War II, most of the resorts were in decline and many of the huge wooden structures eventually succumbed to fire.

But there was nothing up on Blue Ridge Summit except wilderness when the farmhouse was built by John Benchhoof, the son of an immigrant ancestor whose name, date and place of birth, and date of death are still being researched by his descendents.

What is known is that John Benchhoof and his brother, David, owned property in the Blue Ridge Summit area in the early 1800s. John Benchhoof built the farmhouse during this time and lived there until he died in October 1874. John's son, William F. Benchhoof, was likely born in the farmhouse, lived there with his family, and is buried, along with his father, in

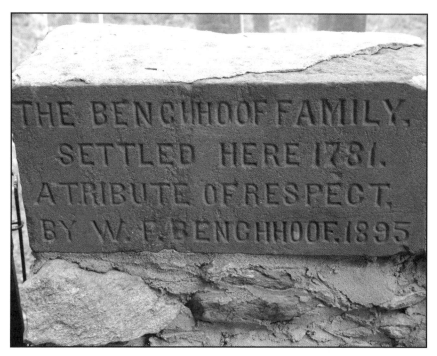

**Benchhoof family tribute.**

athe family graveyard on the farm. A brown stone on the wall surrounding the family graveyard bears the inscription, "The Benchhoof family settled here 1781. A tribute of respect, by W. F. Benchhoof, 1895."

William F. Benchhoof was a provost Marshall during the Civil War; his duties included capturing deserters and recovering stolen government property. Known as the "Colonel," Benchhoof played an active role in developing the area as a summer resort and built his own hotel next to the farmhouse. The resort, named "Montana Springs," burned to the ground some time after the 1920s when the property was sold.

Benchhoof assisted in bringing the Western Maryland Railroad to the area and served as a director of the company. His obituary described him as a "famous hunter" and "a good hater and a warm friend." Benchhoof died January 25, 1896 from "cancer of the face."

## Legends

The story of "Old Devil Bill" has circulated for decades in Blue Ridge Summit. It has never been asserted that the tale refers to any past occupant of the farmhouse in question, however, the name of the protagonist and location of the legend are quite curious.

Old Devil Bill lived on a farm near Charmian, the area adjacent to and synonymous with Blue Ridge Summit on the side of a small mountain. A stone wall enclosed the family graveyard located in front of the barn.

Bill was a heavy drinker, repeatedly beat his timid wife, and rebuffed all who urged him to change his ways. Bill held no fear of the Devil, claiming he could out drink him anytime.

Bill finally got sick one storm-filled night and, in spite of his temperament, neighborhood ladies came in to help with his care. They took turns sitting by the door to his bedroom as everyone in the house waited for him to die. At some point, two large dogs mysteriously made their way into Bill's bedroom. The women tending Bill stared from the doorway at the "two huge dogs, black as the night, their eyes glowing like the hot red coals of Hell."

The women slammed the door shut and dropped to their knees in prayer. Bill died within the hour. At Bill's last breath, the dogs jumped out the bedroom window, carrying Bill's soul to the Devil.

Those present were so frightened that they hurriedly wrapped Bill in his bedclothes and quickly buried him in a shallow grave in the barnyard. His body was later moved to the family graveyard.

To this day, no one can sleep in the room where Old Devil Bill died...as the black, red-eyed dogs return at night to look for him, tearing blankets and sheets from unsuspecting guests. And Old Devil Bill himself still walks the mountain near his home, accompanied by the demon dogs, startling the lost or unwary traveler with his drunken tirades and malevolent companions.

Past owners of the farmhouse repeat a variation of the Old Devil Bill legend:

They claim that what is now a living room on the main floor of the house was once a bedroom, and that a long-ago owner of the house slept there. One day while hunting, the man tangled with a bear, wounding the bear in the process but receiving vicious gashes to his body from the bear's razor-sharp claws. Weak and bleeding, he made his way home and collapsed onto his bed.

Sometime during the night, the bear, smelling the homeowner's blood, burst in through the door and dragged the man out into the night. His body was never found.

## Ghostly Occurrences

Colorful stories aside, throughout the years, owners of the house in Blue Ridge Summit and their guests have reported firsthand experiences with unseen company. Phantom footsteps and the occasional whiff of tobacco smoke are common. Some guests have refused to sleep in the small, back bedroom on the third floor while others have felt uneasy in the hallway between the two bedrooms. None have ever wandered at night to the family graveyard on the property. Although newly restored, with trimmed plots and a re-pointed rock wall, the old headstones radiate unease.

## *Apparitions*

The house is filled with apparitions, impressions, and energies layered over one another like pages in a photograph album, stretching back over more than one hundred years. Many souls have come and gone from the old farmhouse, many births and deaths have taken place within its walls. Original stone walls hiding behind new paneling, slanted support beams, and sloping wooden floors replay their past. Some of the energies dominate while others flash briefly, causing a variety of manifestations... *some seen, some heard, some smelled, and some felt.*

The following apparitions are merely the strongest.

### **The First Floor**

A porch on the first floor of the farmhouse grants entry through a door that opens into the middle of the room. A massive fireplace is built into the wall to the right. Support beams embedded in the ceiling are bowed but sturdy. Original stone walls lay exposed in the laundry room behind the main room. A thin, winding staircase carries the visitor to the rest of the house.

Activity animates the air.

A persistent droning sound caused by hundreds of bees registers in the barely perceptible range of hearing. The bees are not in the house but are outside...in bee colonies someone is tending.

This floor of the house might have served as the kitchen at one time because the fireplace is lit and there is a woman standing in front of it, stirring something in a huge, black pot. The boiling liquid in the pot is beige or yellow and might be soap.

Her dark hair with some wisps of grey is pulled back into a tight bun. She has a full, round face with a little bit of a point to her chin and bright red lips. Her face and expression are friendly and she seems very happy.

She's wearing a grey or light brown dress that appears to be cotton, but the material itches. The dress is tight across her ample bosom and the long sleeves are very fitted. The skirt is billowy and flowing.

She stands approximately five feet tall, is thirty-six years old, married, and very happy. Her name or part of her name might be Ann.

Her husband works at something that involves money. Paper records surround him and he records information in a ledger. The pages are cream-colored, unlined, and he turns them over after he writes on them. The ledger is very neat and not fingered. He uses a pen and an inkwell and works at a desk.

He is very thin and is several inches taller than his wife. He has a beard but no moustache.

He is wearing a black morning coat made from a polished wool material. Although not necessarily an unhappy man, he is always quite serious; the exact opposite of his wife. Even in appearance they are opposites: he, sharp and angular, she, jovial and round.

Who they might be and at what time they lived is unknown, but their mood is calm and content...very unlike the aura of the other floors.

## The Second Floor

The second floor contains the living room and the current kitchen. A door off the kitchen leads outside to the back of the house. This area was clearly not used as a kitchen when the house was built. The atmosphere is reminiscent of an office and this was the area where people were paid.

Tobacco smoke fills the air inside the house from the men gathering by the back door. They come in and mill about, waiting and smoking. They are not all directly associated with the farmstead, but appear to work in the area. Entering and exiting in large numbers, the men stomp around in dirty boots as they exchange loud greetings. Other men are sitting at a large wooden table in the middle of the room. This table exceeds the current area of the kitchen, extending over into the area where the living room is. All of the men are farmers or laborers wearing simple clothing that's worn and dirty from time spent digging and hauling. They are all there to be paid and are growing impatient.

The faint buzzing of the bees is heard over their voices.

Nothing is felt in the current living room. If this was once a bedroom where devil dogs kept vigil or where a man was taken by animals, the house is not telling.

## The Third Floor

### Bathroom and First Bedroom

The third floor bears witness to most of the energy in the house. Bedrooms are currently located here and are believed to have been used as such since the house was built.

A bathroom has been added to the third floor, taking space from what had been a large bedroom, and is located at the top of the twisting staircase. The sound of bees seeps in through the front wall of the house. There is a little girl here, playing in what used to be part of the bedroom.

She is wearing a long, light grey woolen skirt. The skirt is full, not straight, and she has a small white apron on over the skirt. A white day cap conceals her hair except for the light brown bangs that rest on her forehead beneath it. The cap resembles a plain bonnet with a small peak. Possibly made of muslin, the back of the cap is perfectly round as it sits on the young girl's head.

She looks to be around six or seven years old, and her name has a "G" sound in it, either her first name or last name, or perhaps a name associated with her in some fashion.

She is playing with a cornhusk doll and something that looks like a stuffed horse. The face has been painted on and the husk dress feathers out from the cob. The horse toy is stuffed with horsehair. It's not as primitive looking as the cornhusk doll and appears to have been manufactured. The little stuffed horse is her prized possession.

The young, happy, healthy girl is in stark contrast to a boy in the bedroom, who dates from another era and has no association with the girl in time. The boy, lying listlessly on the bed, is near death and his mother, hovering nearby, isn't feeling well, either.

The doors to the two bedrooms on this floor intersect at the hallway. This is the point of highest paranormal activity in the house and rarely has anyone walked into either bedroom from this place in the hallway without feeling a sudden chill.

The boy lies in a small bed pushed up against the wall of the larger bedroom to the right. His mother stands in the doorway between the two bedrooms and paces from one bedroom to the other and back.

She is distressed and doesn't know what to do. Her husband has left her alone with their very sick child.

It might be around 1846-49 and many people in the area were coming down with this illness. The source of the sickness was the drinking water.

The boy is short and stocky. His name or a name associated with him has an "Al" sound to it, such as Alexander, Alan, Alfred, or Albert and he is eight to ten years old. He has a round, full face and a ruddy complexion, but it's blood red right now and incredibly hot as he lies soaked in sweat from fever. The skin on his face is taunt and shiny, almost like the skin of a balloon. It looks as if his face is ready to explode.

If the little boy had been well, he would have been dressed in clothing resembling that of a present-day Mennonite: plain, very dark trousers with suspenders, and a white shirt that has taken on an off-white or beige appearance, with buttons down the front and a tab collar opened into a "v" at the neck. The linen shirt is scratchy. He carries a red handkerchief or scarf with him. The red material is imprinted with white designs: lacy loops and star patterns, and a white border along the edge.

The woman watching over him is not feeling well herself. For some reason, her husband is absent. It's not that he has divorced or left her, but at this particular time she is home alone with their sick son. He isn't away at work, either. Whatever he is doing, it has taken him away from the house for an extended period of time and she cannot get a message to him. She chastises him under her breath. She is beside herself as she paces back and forth, walking through the thresholds of the adjacent bedrooms. She looks out the back window and sees that the doctor has arrived. Eventually her own illness will cause her to weaken, and she will drag a rocking chair into the room where she will stay day and night, watching over her very sick child.

The doctor arrives in an elongated and elaborately decorated wagon. The wagon resembles a buckboard that has been customized to act as a hearse because the doctor is also the undertaker. The body of the wagon behind the bench seat upon which the doctor sits is fully enclosed by a large, box-like cabin. The front of the cabin is cut into an arch that comes down to form columns on each side. The sides of the compartment bow out a little and the top is a solid, heavy square. The wood from which the wagon has been crafted is painted a glossy black and bears gold leaf designs. The bench seat is covered with red felt held in place by tuxedo buttons.

The doctor/undertaker appears to be five feet six or seven inches tall, has a thin build, and a somewhat long beard. He is always formally dressed. He wears a black felt stovepipe hat with a satin band around the base were the brim begins. He wears a dark suit and a very white, flimsy billowy shirt. A large, floppy bow tie hangs out from the front of his jacket.

He came here as a doctor and tried to administer to the little boy, but the boy was too weak by then to overcome his illness.

### Second Bedroom

The second bedroom on the third floor, the smaller one down the hall along the back wall of the house, broadcasts the most intense energy. Along with the hallway between the thresholds of the two bedroom doors, guests and residents have felt uncomfortable in the room, believing they were being watched and not alone. Chills and strange sounds from the closet are common.

A young girl, thirteen or fourteen years old, watches out the back window for her sweetheart, a young man just a few years older who lives in a house she can see from her window. They have known each other all their lives and although they are too young to get married, there is no doubt they someday will. The young girl is connected in some way to the older woman by the fireplace in the basement.

She has dark hair pulled back into a braid and curls along the sides of her face. Her dark dress has a scalloped neck edged with lace. At this moment she is happy, but she is concerned about a war. While she does not feel that the war is imminent, she fears it will eventually end up in her backyard. But her biggest concern at this moment is the young man who has won her heart. He has told her he thinks he wants to go and fight in the war.

She believes she will be able to use her powers of persuasion to convince him not to go.

But she will fail.

A short time later, her energy subsides into heartbreak and anger. She is in despair. Her intended had wanted a "distraction," something to do before they got married. She believed the war would be more than a mere "distraction" and tried everything she knew to change his mind, but he did not listen. He went off to war and never came back.

The air in the room is filled with her cries: I *told* you so! I *told* you not to do this and look what happened! My life is *ruined* because you're not here! The words are thick with pain. She paces and clenches her fists and cries bitterly, her shoulders quaking with the fury of her sorrow. Her lost joy and perpetual sorrow clash in the charged atmosphere of the bedroom. The energy is static and sharp.

The young woman never married and spent the rest of her life mourning the fact that the love of her life did not listen to her. He went away, and never returned.

Despair snatches the breath of those she touches.

# Epilogue

The Benchhoof (later changed to Benchoff) family archives indicate many possibilities for the apparitions detailed above. One descendant in particular was known for the beehives he tended on the property, possibly accounting for the buzzing sounds heard throughout the house. While interesting, no attempt is made here to identify any energy or explain any phenomenon. Such speculation is left to the discretion of` the reader.

The farmstead in Blue Ridge Summit well exceeds its past glory. Restored structures and manicured grounds greet the living with warmth and peace. Prior inhabitants appear to go about their business unnoticed except for an occasional sensation, sound, or smell, and the once-in-a-while movement of a neglected closet door.

**Benchhoof family gravesite, Blue Ridge Summit.**

# 8

# The Allison-Antrim Museum

### 365 South Ridge Avenue,
### Greencastle, Pennsylvania

When the house at 365 South Ridge Avenue in Greencastle went up for sale in early 1988, Jeanette Bearfoot was living on the second floor of a funeral home. Her uncle had owned a funeral home so the location did not strike her as unusual and the accommodations were adequate for her and her husband, Robert May, and their two children, Jarrod, 7, and Emily, 5. But they were in search of a home in Franklin County and the house on South Ridge Avenue, although badly in need of renovation and cosmetic repair, went on the market while they were looking and seemed to them ideal.

They bought it in the spring and gutted it completely before moving in...that was what probably started *it*.

Robert May went to the empty house in the evenings to work on small projects. All seemed to go well in the beginning, but then he began to feel as if he were not alone...that something was watching, peering over his shoulder as he went about the house at night. He stayed, ignoring these feelings. Then the night came when his pager went off and the message screen was blank. He stayed and continued his work. Moments later the pager went off again, the screen remained blank, and he felt *something* watching him. He later explained to his wife that he had an "overwhelming feeling" that he had to get out of there.

He stopped going alone to the house at night.

**The Allison-Antrim Museum, Greencastle.**

A decade later, when the house had been sold again and was in the process of being converted for use as the Allison-Antrim Museum, Kenneth Shockey was standing on a ladder in the central hallway and felt the same thing look at him. It was evening and he had stopped by to change some light bulbs in the hallway fixtures. He was almost on the top step of the ladder. As he reached up to put in the new bulb, he felt *it*...just behind his shoulder, almost breathing, almost touching the back of his neck.

The ladder shook as he stumbled down. He left the light bulb and the hallway and fled.

He doesn't go alone to the house at night anymore, either.

## Ghostly Occurrences

Emily's bedroom was on the second floor at the top of the stairs. Her bed was placed so that when she looked out into the hallway, she could see the wall at the top of the staircase. They had been in the house for only a few weeks when Emily told her mother about the face on the wall.

"She wasn't afraid or anything," Jeanette recalled. "She matter-of-factly said there was a face on the wall at the top of the stairs. She described it as a face with red eyes."

Jeanette didn't press her young daughter for details as she didn't want to frighten her, but she found Emily's description of the face disturbing and discussed with some friends the possibility of getting the house blessed by a Catholic priest.

Before any action was taken, the problem appeared to resolve itself.

"About a week later, my husband and I were down in the kitchen and we heard this upstairs window just slam shut," Jeanette explained. They believed it to have been a window on the second floor. "After that, Emily never saw it again."

But Emily *saw* other things.

## Emily's Bedroom

During the ten years that she and her family occupied the house, Emily had always felt that there was a "presence" of some sort in her room. "I always kind of felt when I went to sleep there was something right around me," she recalled. "I felt like something was touching my head, or my covers. It would touch my hair." Emily spoke to it sometimes out of nervousness. "I was always uncomfortable walking around the house at night."

They had several cats that had the run of the house. One of the cats spent most of its time in Emily's room. It would sit and stare at something none of them could see.

Electronic devices would malfunction in Emily's room. Her radio and television would turn on and off at different hours of the day and night. Her father bought her a telephone for her room one Christmas. The phone rang at night. "No one would ever be there," Emily said. "I kind of always knew it was the ghost."

## The Figure in the Hallway

The upstairs bathroom is located just to the right of the attic door. While Emily was brushing her teeth one night, she glanced through the open bathroom door to the hallway and saw a figure walking toward the attic. Emily described the apparition as a young woman.

"I did a double take," she explained. "I *know* I saw *something*. I was pretty freaked out."

**Staircase, Allison-Antrim Museum.**

Emily slept in her parents' bedroom that night. "I told my Mom I just saw a ghost."

Years later, when they were older, Emily would find out that her brother's friend had seen the mysterious young woman, too.

## Visitors

When Jeanette's niece came to visit, she told her aunt that she felt very uncomfortable in the living room side of the house. Although they had a sofa bed there, she would not sleep in it. She would not sleep in Emily's room, either. "She felt that there was someone in the house watching over us who didn't like intruders," Jeanette recounted. Whatever it was sensed that her niece was not part of the immediate family. And *it* didn't want her there. "The feeling was really, really strong."

## Unexplained Events

Although the blinds would be left at the same level on all the windows of a given room, should the house be left vacant for a time, the blinds would somehow roll themselves up or let themselves down. This happened in all of the rooms.

On the South Ridge Avenue side of the house there are two doors, one of which enters directly into the dining room. This door locks with a skeleton key and is protected on the outside by a storm door. The Mays never used this door and always kept it locked.

Jeanette found the door and the storm door unlocked a number of times when no one had been in the house.

Lights turned off at night would be on in the morning. Lights turned on in the evening would turn themselves off.

While reading one quiet summer's night, Jeanette heard the sound of children laughing. She had put her own children to bed hours ago and knew immediately it wasn't them, but the more she listened the more she couldn't really tell where it was coming from. The

**Latch on attic door, Allison-Antrim Museum.**

laughter came from "everywhere and nowhere." She looked outside in the boxwoods that lined the entrance. She listened to the rooms of the house. The source was never found.

The latch on the attic door seemed to make noise sometimes. Emily and her friends played in the attic. Sometimes they found themselves locked in the attic when no one else was home.

A shed at the rear of the property served as a playhouse. Sometimes the children would find themselves locked in there as well.

During the years that the Mays occupied the house, there were no walnut trees in the yard, but walnuts were always everywhere.

Emily claims to have had walnuts thrown at her while playing in the yard. It was not a windy day and no one had been around. At least two walnuts struck her, tossed at her by an unseen hand.

Items would go missing or appear to have been moved while other items appeared to have a mind of their own: earrings disappeared from the kitchen counter; VHS tapes left their storage and were found wedged between items of furniture; a music box in the room next to the living room would play by itself; an antique chalk figurine sitting safely on the top shelf of a bookcase in this same room somehow managed to smash itself during the night, unheard, and was found shattered on the floor in the morning.

~~~~~~~

Bonnie A. Shockey, president of the Allison-Antrim Museum, and her husband Kenneth B. Shockey have already experienced enough unexplained events to know they are not alone in the house. Although not malevolent in any way, the mischievous energies occasionally startle and surprise them.

A mysterious "knocking" sound can be heard when one of them is on the second floor in one of the rooms and no longer visible from the hallway on the first floor. It's as if a curious entity, confined to the first floor, is annoyed that it is not being attended to. It is possible this is the same curious entity that peers over the shoulders of anyone working in the main hallway and staircase area.

The latch on the lock to the attic door can be heard jiggling and the door has locked itself.

The blinds continue to go up or down on their own. No one attempts to align them anymore, as they are never found the way they are left.

The Shockeys ensure that all lights are off when they leave the museum. Patrons walking by at night have noticed lights on in some of the rooms and, on at least one occasion, all the lights were on.

A few years ago, artwork commemorating the anniversary of 9/11 from Greencastle Area Senior High School was displayed in the parlor on the walls and on a presentation screen. It was a Saturday morning and Bonnie was alone in the house, working upstairs, when she heard what sounded like furniture being moved. She came downstairs and found that some of the pictures had been removed from the screen and the walls, and were resting on the floor. Bonnie surmised that perhaps they had "slid off" in some manner. She put them back up and went upstairs. It wasn't long before she heard the sound again—like furniture being moved. She came downstairs and looked around, but nothing had been disturbed. She returned upstairs and, after several minutes, heard the sounds again. She came down. Nothing. Bonnie retrieved a screwdriver from a tool kit "in case someone was there" and called her husband to come over and keep her company.

# Before It Was A Museum

### "My Walnut Hill Property"

Alexander L. Irwin was born September 15, 1811 in Northern Ireland and died September 22, 1890 in Greencastle. He purchased the land and built the house that came to be known in April 1998 as the Allison-Antrim Museum. Historical records reviewed and maintained by the Museum indicate Irwin was a prominent merchant who in the 1850s established Greencastle's first hardware store. The house faces south because in 1860 when the house was built, Leitersburg Pike was the main road and South Ridge Avenue did not yet exist. In his will, Irwin described his residence and the lands surrounding it as, "My Walnut Hill Property."

Irwin lived in the house with his second wife, Martha J. Means. Together they had five children, four of whom lived to adulthood and none of whom appear to have married. Their last surviving child, Sarah Annie, lived in the house until her death there in December 1933.

There are those who believe Annie still walks amongst those who visit the Allison-Antrim Museum and that it was her presence that Emily May felt in her room and glimpsed in the hallway as she brushed her teeth that night. Some have felt a chill in the room that now displays childrens' toys and artifacts, particularly in front of the windows that look out across the lawn. Some believe they have seen her.

Sarah Annie has been described as wearing a light colored dress with large, puffed shoulders and a ruffle collar edged with blue piping. The sleeves are long and gathered in ruffles displaying the same blue piping at the wrists. The dress has a blue sash and there

**The Allison-Antrim Museum.**

is a large ruffle around the bottom of the dress with a grosgrain or ribbon-like trim.

Her shoes appear more like boots, rising up over her ankles. Black with brownish tan buttons, they are pointy and narrow and have a tiny heel.

Her hair is very light brown with almost orange-red highlights. She wears it down with a ribbon in back. She does not appear to have naturally curly hair, as it is wavier at the bottom than at the top.

She is young and incredibly pretty.

She seems to be waiting for a man, a man who has been seen walking across the lawn and looking up at the windows of the second floor. During an evening event at the Museum, a guest commented on the outstanding costume worn by a man seen outside, someone they thought Museum officials had hired.

This man has been described as wearing a light tan or grey suit with a white shirt, black tie, and sometimes carrying, sometimes wearing a round, derby-like hat. The jacket is short and the pants

**Annie's room, Allison-Antrim Museum.**

are tight with buttons down the lower leg area. His boots rise above the ankle. The pants and jacket match, and he seems to be wearing something resembling a cummerbund. He is somewhat chubby with a ruddy complexion to his very round face and appears to be very happy.

It's believed that the Irwin children, their relatives, and friends played throughout the house, but particularly in the attic, where sometimes their giggling and footsteps are still heard today, and where sometimes the door is playfully locked.

## Epilogue

There are no walnut trees on the property anymore, but it does appear their presence remains in the walnuts found periodically on the grounds and mysteriously thrown at past residents. And it is also apparent that the Irwin children still play in the attic and on the grounds, giggling and locking the attic door. And Sarah Annie, as a young woman, anxiously waits by her bedroom window, looking out at the lawn where a young man is walking toward the house to call on her.

# 9

# The White Lady

## White Ladies Everywhere

T he White Lady gets around. She is absolutely everywhere. She is in Great Britain, she is in Ireland, she is in Brazil and Portugal, she is in the Czech Republic, she is in Malta and the Philippines, Finland, and Bulgaria. Just about every country on the planet boasts a ghost called The White Lady.

In the United Sates, she inhabits at least one town in every state, if not several towns or cemeteries, fields, or roads. She can be seen at night or during the day. She is always alone, always ethereal, and always does her laundry since her clothes, gown, or whatever flowing garment she is wearing is always a pure, gleaming white.

The White Lady is a feminine ghostly presence that has suffered some unspeakable trauma. Some legends have her losing a child in either a swimming or boating accident, which causes her to wander along lakes or streams. Or she is believed to have died the night before or on the day of her wedding and is haunting houses or halls in search of her fiancée. Other legends claim she and her fiancée died in different places at different times and now haunt separate locations, each one searching for the other. Sometimes she is a murder victim. Sometimes she is an accident victim. The variations are endless, but the consistent theme is that she is *dressed in white* and is searching or waiting for someone.

Franklin County is home to at least two White Lady phenomena; one in Pond Bank and one in South Mountain, along Loop Road.

## The White Lady of Pond Bank

The tiny community of Pond Bank is located between Mont Alto and Chambersburg on Route 997, at the intersection of White Rock and Duffield roads. It's a small cluster of houses bordered by Penn National Golf Course and the well-tended lawns of the surrounding golf course community on the south, farmlands on the north and west, and Michaux State Forest on the east. Pond Bank got its name from the many ponds that formed there in the aftermath of iron ore mining in the early 1800s. Huge trenches and ditches from which the ore had been extracted became filled with water, fed either by underground springs or from runoff, creating numerous ponds.

Sightings of the White Lady have typically been reported along Route 997 or in the rolling fields just north of the intersection of White Rock and Duffield roads.

A current resident of Pond Bank moved here more than fifteen years ago from the neighboring town of Waynesboro. She related that when she told neighbors she was moving to Pond Bank, they immediately warned her about the White Lady. They told her that a woman, dressed in white, hides in the woods or under a bridge along the road. As an unsuspecting driver passes by, she suddenly leaps onto the hood of the car. Police have heard the same tale over and over, responding to shaken drivers who have driven off the road into the drainage ditches.

"A fellow my sister was dating stopped going out with her when we moved up here because he didn't want to come to Pond Bank," she said. Her sister's boyfriend claimed he had seen the White Lady one night while driving home on Route 997. He had just passed a wooded area when he glimpsed her out of the corner of his eye, walking along the side of the road. She was dressed in a white, flowing gown that glowed with its own source of illumination. The next thing he knew, she was clinging to the hood of his car. He slammed on his brakes and, as the car swerved, the White Lady slid off and disappeared. "He said that when he got home, he actually had fingernail marks on the side of his car where she had slid off."

Another resident recalled the story of three children who were playing in a field by the state forestlands. It was dusk and a woman dressed all in white suddenly emerged from the surrounding woods. She appeared to be wearing a gown or long dress and, as she slowly moved toward them, the children saw that she was not walking but actually floating a few inches above the ground. The terrified children fled and never returned to the field.

Adults hiking through the state forest in the vicinity of the same field, which is near an abandoned quarry now filled with water, have also reported seeing someone or something moving among the trees, wearing something white. Upon further inspection, the apparition is always female, but disappears moments after being seen.

Various legends surround the origin of the White Lady of Pond Bank. One tale claims that sometime around the turn of the century, a woman committed murder-suicide, drowning herself and her infant child for unknown reasons, in one of the ponds for which Pond Bank was named. Filled with remorse for what she has done, she returns at night, searching for her child. Sometimes she rides on the hoods of cars or in the beds of pickup trucks, searching to see if her infant has been taken by vehicles passing on the road.

According to another story, a man took his young son fishing

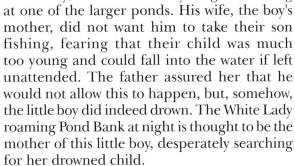

at one of the larger ponds. His wife, the boy's mother, did not want him to take their son fishing, fearing that their child was much too young and could fall into the water if left unattended. The father assured her that he would not allow this to happen, but, somehow, the little boy did indeed drown. The White Lady roaming Pond Bank at night is thought to be the mother of this little boy, desperately searching for her drowned child.

Still another tale takes the action a short distance away from the center of Pond Bank and focuses on the quarry pond along the state forest lands. The quarry was once a huge pit that eventually became flooded when the miners struck underground springs. The miners, working down in the pit when the waters burst through, drowned. One of these workers was engaged to be married and the White Lady roaming this area at night is assumed to be his grieving fiancée.

Another story involves a runaway wagon that is said to have flipped over alongside the Pond Bank quarry, tossing its occupants, a young married couple, into the cold, deep water where they drowned. According to this version of events, the White Lady is the young bride, searching frantically for her husband in the woods and fields near the bank of the pond where they both died.

**One of the many ponds in Pond Bank.**

## *The White Lady of South Mountain*

Up on South Mountain, an old tale of unknown origin explains why many horse owners are surprised to discover that a section of a horse's mane somehow comes to be plaited overnight in a smooth, well-formed braid while the rest of the mane remains wild and uncombed. It's said that witches form the plaits. Witches wander through the barns and fields and find horses that have not been cared for and play with their manes at night. Left unattended, the braid is said to increase in length until it wraps itself around the horse's neck and chokes the animal to death.

But the most common legend shared among the inhabitants of this small, rural town on the eastern boundary of Franklin County is that of the White Lady.

No one knows where she came from. No stories tell of her origin, but many of the long-time residents of South Mountain have *seen* her and have come to accept her as one of their own.

For decades a woman dressed in a long white gown or robe has been seen walking along Loop Road. Sometimes a small white dog accompanies her. She treads along one side of Loop Road, but never crosses it. She has also been seen in fields near the road, ambling aimlessly, her white clothing gently billowing in an unfelt wind.

She was seen during the days when the primary mode of transportation on the mountain was a horse-drawn cart. People on horseback, driving by in vehicles, or on foot have seen her through the years. She is solid in appearance...an apparition with form and shadow. But then she turns away and disappears.

Nearly all the residents of South Mountain have at least one family member who has seen her. As they are with their own kin, they are protective of her. They do not approach, as she seems quite preoccupied with something, never apparently noticing those who watch her. And they do not flee, as she is no threat to them.

Perhaps someday she will find her way to the other side of Loop Road. Until then, she might be seen at dusk, strolling benignly through the mist with her small, white dog, unaware of the world around her, wandering, if even momentarily, from wherever her soul has gone.

# 10

## Toll House #2

O ut on Route 30 West in the rural hamlet of St. Thomas, approximately five miles west of Chambersburg, the front door of a scarred stone house watches vehicles speed by only inches away. There had been a porch in front of the door at one time and a long gate that reached the porch from the other side of the road. A century or so ago, no one traveled east or west on the road in front of this house without stopping at the gate to pay the toll. Stripped now of its gate and porch, it sits like a stone monolith, barely noticed in the overgrown brush surrounding it. No one glancing at this humble structure today could possibly imagine the link this house provides to the entire history of the United States or to well known events and the famous people whose efforts during their separate, unconnected lives fused to produce the present.

It all began January 1, 1745, in Chester County, Pennsylvania, just outside Philadelphia, with the birth of the only son of Isaac and Elizabeth Wayne on the family homestead known as Waynesborough. The infant would grow into a man whose forceful personality, strategic military skills, and fearless dedication to his country would brand him in history as "Mad" Anthony Wayne. He would become one of the most colorful commanders in the Continental Army.

But his exploits in life pale in comparison to the tales he has spawned in death.

**Toll House #2.**

# "Mad" Anthony Wayne

Anthony Wayne has the distinction of having had a county, nine townships, and three boroughs named after him in the Commonwealth of Pennsylvania alone. There is a Wayne County in thirteen states, Wayne City in Illinois, towns of Waynesville in North Carolina and Missouri, and scores of other cities, towns, political jurisdictions, and institutions named after him.

Legend has it that sometime during the Revolutionary War, Anthony Wayne, while watering his horse at a stream near what would one day become the borough of Waynesboro, commented, "What a beautiful place to build a town." But it is more than likely that Anthony Wayne never even set foot in or near Waynesboro, Pennsylvania.

Scotsman John Wallace originally named his 633 acres and 119 perches Mt. Vernon when he settled in current Waynesboro about 1749. His homestead was called Wallacetown and was conveyed to his son Robert upon his death. Eventually Robert's brother John obtained the land and it was he who, in 1797, decided to lay out a town and name it after his commanding officer in the Revolutionary War. Wallace had served under Anthony Wayne in the Battle of Stony Point, New York, in July 1779 and was a devoted admirer of his commander. As a result of Wallace's efforts, the town was named Waynesburg when first incorporated in 1818. However, the federal government prohibited post offices in one state from having the same name and Waynesburg (another town in Western Pennsylvania) had already been taken. Eventually reincorporated as Waynesborough, the name was shortened to Waynesboro in 1831.

And even though the town is named after him, Anthony Wayne doesn't haunt there—that's probably because his energy is already stretched to the limit, given the number of places he already allegedly frequents.

## *The Revolutionary War*

Prior to the outbreak of the Revolutionary War, Anthony Wayne worked as a surveyor, tannery operator, and legislator, representing Chester County in the Pennsylvania General Assembly from 1774 to 1775. When war was declared, he raised a militia and was appointed colonel of the Fourth Regiment of Pennsylvania troops. In the spring of 1776, he and his regiment were sent to Canada to reinforce the Canadian expedition, the ill-fated attempt by Congress to gain another colony for the United States. Wayne was wounded at the Battle of Three Rivers. His actions in battle gained him a promotion to brigadier general in February 1777.

Wayne led troops in every major battle of the Revolutionary War, but is probably best known for his stunning victory in the Battle of Stony Point in New York State. In the spring of 1779, Wayne was placed in charge of an elite corps of light infantry hand-picked from various units from various states. On July 16, 1779, he led his troops in a nocturnal surprise attack on the British forces entrenched at Stony Point. The fort, military supplies, cannons, and more than five hundred prisoners were captured. Wayne was awarded the Congressional Gold Medal for his efforts. Widespread respect for his military skills and judgment earned him the dubious honor of being tasked to lead forces in the most difficult and challenging conflicts for the duration of the war. He retired from the army in 1783 with the rank of brevet-major general.

Wayne did not achieve the accolades or successes in his civilian life that he had in his military career. He served in the Pennsylvania General Assembly for a year and then moved to Georgia. He lost the estate given to him by the state of Georgia for his military service to foreclosure and then lost his elected seat in Congress because of irregularities in the Georgia election.

Wayne was, therefore, probably ecstatic when President George Washington called him back to military service.

## The Battle of Fallen Timbers

The Treaty of Paris in 1783 was supposed to have brought an end to the hostilities following the War for Independence; however, this would prove not to be the case.

Although the territory south of the Great Lakes had been ceded to the United States, it was inhabited by Indians who, for the most part, had sided with the British in the Revolutionary War. The Indian tribes had not been consulted when the Treaty of Paris was signed and they resisted annexation. Furthermore, Britain refused to evacuate fortifications in the region and encouraged the Indians to harass the Americans.

President George Washington attempted to quell the growing violence in the northwest, but a confederation of Miami, Shawnee, Lenape, and Wyandot Indians had succeeded in winning major victories over United States forces in 1790 and 1791.

Faced with stunning military defeats in an area vital to the expansion and economic survival of the newly formed United States, Washington called Wayne out of retirement in 1792 and appointed him major general and commander-in-chief of the new American army. Wayne recruited and created a well-disciplined force that defeated the Indian confederacy at the Battle of Fallen Timbers in what is present-day Maumee, Ohio, on August 20, 1794. Wayne then negotiated the Treaty of Greenville, which, when signed on August 3, 1795, officially ended the Northwest Indian War.

Although hostilities would continue in the region for decades, the end of the Northwest Indian War opened the floodgates for westward migration as Americans spread out over their expanding country.

Although completely inconceivable at the time, and ignored by most today, the highway system that would evolve some one hundred years later and the toll houses built because of it were, in fact, born in Wayne's victory at Fallen Timbers.

## "*Mad*"

The origin of the nickname "Mad" Anthony Wayne has several possibilities. These include Wayne's legendary bad temper, his recklessness and daring in battle, the ramblings of a drunken disgruntled soldier, or the head wound he received at the Battle of Stony Point, which eventually resulted in epileptic-type seizures causing Wayne to foam at the mouth.

The "nom de guerre" may or may not have suited Wayne in life; however, the events surrounding the eventual resting place, or places, of his remains would definitely have garnered Wayne's fury. He likely would have embraced the title had he known what was going to happen to him.

## *His Death and Burial*

Jay's Treaty of 1795, named for American statesman John Jay who negotiated the treaty with Britain, dealt with the escalating conflict between the two countries following the conclusion of the Revolutionary War. Under the terms of this treaty, Britain agreed to withdraw from posts on United States soil it had continued to hold after the war.

Wayne, ordered to occupy these posts in 1796, was returning from a trip to a military post in Detroit when he was stricken with gout. He arrived by boat at Fort Presque Isle, now Erie, Pennsylvania, November 19, 1796 and was taken to the quarters of the military commander for treatment.

Doctor John C. Wallace was summoned from Pittsburgh, more than one hundred miles away. Unfortunately, the gout reached Wayne's stomach and he suffered horrible pains. He died December 15, 1796. Wayne was just fifty-six years old. Dr. Wallace arrived the day he died.

Wayne was buried in his uniform, in a plain, wooden casket, at the foot of the flagstaff of the post's blockhouse. His initials, age, and date of death were driven into the top of the coffin with brass tacks.

Twelve years later, Wayne's daughter, Margaretta, pleaded with her brother, Isaac, to travel to Erie, retrieve the remains of their father, and bring them home to Radnor, Pennsylvania so that they could be buried in the family's plot. Margaretta was seriously ill at the time, so it's likely Isaac agreed to this endeavor to calm her. At any rate, he set out for Erie in a small, two-wheeled horse-drawn carriage know as a "sulky." He should have realized before he left that there was no way a full-sized casket was ever going to fit into a one-seat carriage.

Isaac enlisted the assistance of Dr. Wallace, the same physician who had traveled from Pittsburgh to tend to his dying father, to arrange the disinterment. Witnesses to the opening of the casket claimed that Wayne's body was almost perfectly preserved. The body had the consistency of chalk and only one leg was decayed.

Dr. Wallace came up with a solution to the problem of space in the sulky. Using a custom then common to American Indians, he dismembered the body and boiled it in a large kettle until the flesh dropped off. The bones were scraped clean and put into a trunk for transport. The flesh, knives, and instruments used in the procedure were placed into the original casket and re-interred.

Isaac successfully returned to Radnor with the bones of his father. The bones were afforded an appropriate ceremony and buried at St. David's Episcopal Church July 4, 1809.

Back in Erie, the abandoned blockhouse burned down in 1853 and the land around it was leveled. It wasn't until 1878 that Wayne's first gravesite was rediscovered. The badly rotted coffin was dug up again and the coffin lid bearing the identifying brass tacks, remnants of clothing, and the dissection instruments were recovered and are now on display at the Erie County Historical Society. The Commonwealth of Pennsylvania rebuilt the blockhouse as a memorial to Wayne on the grounds of the Pennsylvania Soldiers and Sailors Home in Erie.

The kettle has never been found.

Legend has it that Isaac ran into major problems trying to get the trunk containing his father's bones from Erie to Radnor. Riding in his small sulky, Isaac traveled over 380 miles on unpaved roads on what is now Route 322. The rough ride caused the large trunk to keep falling out of the carriage. It would smash to the ground and break open, scattering bones along the road in the process. Isaac tried to retrieve them all, but missed a few. Another version suggests that Isaac was in such a hurry to get home that he did not notice the bones falling out of the trunk along the way.

Thus it is said that on every New Year's Day, Wayne's birthday, somewhere along Route 322, "Mad" Anthony Wayne can be seen astride his horse, dressed in full military regalia, riding across the state in search of his missing bones.

Wayne is alleged to haunt several other locations as well, all of which figure predominately in the Revolutionary War. He is frequently seen on horseback and always dressed in military attire. These locations include the battlefields at Chadd's Ford, Pennsylvania, and Fort Ticonderoga and Stony Point in New York.

Perhaps someday he will alter his route and stop by the old Toll House that still stands on Lincoln Highway in St. Thomas.

# The National Road

Thanks to "Mad" Anthony Wayne, the Treaty of Greenville ended the Northwest Indian War and opened the Ohio and Northwest Territories to westward expansion. People, trade, and business began to move west, but the Appalachian Mountains remained a formidable barrier to travel. By the end of the eighteenth century, the need for construction of a roadway over the mountains and across the country was critical to commercial interests. Without a viable route from the eastern seaboard to the west, businesses could not survive and the population west of the mountains would see shortages of supplies and food.

In 1806, legislation to construct the nation's first multi-state, federally funded highway, later known as the National Road, was passed. Construction began in 1811 in Cumberland, Maryland and the roadway was eventually completed as far as Wheeling, in what is now West Virginia, by 1818. The National Road served as the model for interstate roads and turnpikes that would eventually crisscross the country.

Ownership of the National Road passed to the states in the 1830s. Now known as the National Pike, states began to erect tollhouses along their portion in order to collect fees for maintenance purposes. Travel essentially exploded along the Pike, bringing with it an increase in stagecoach lines, stables, taverns, hotels, and other businesses catering to a population on the move.

The Chambersburg and Bedford Turnpike was constructed during the early 1800s, with tollhouses spaced fifteen miles apart. Taverns sprang up every few miles or so along this route, but were still insufficient to meet the demands of travelers—as many as one hundred horses might be stationed at a single tavern at any given time.

By the 1850s, railroad transportation began to overtake roadways as the preferred means of travel. Stagecoach lines

began to go out of business and tollhouses closed as the number of passengers declined. Eventually the toll roads fell into disuse and disrepair. Many tollhouses were converted to residences or demolished.

The invention and perfection of the automobile renewed the need for viable roadways and an interstate system facilitating rapid and safe travel. In 1913, a group of businessmen from the automotive industry formed the Lincoln Highway Association to push for the creation of a publicly funded road that would stretch from New York City to San Francisco. In Pennsylvania, the Chambersburg and Bedford Turnpike became part of the Lincoln Highway, later known as Route 30, one of the primary roads bisecting Franklin County.

The remaining tollhouse on the former Chambersburg and Bedford Turnpike, now Route 30, is known as Toll House #2. There is conflicting information as to when it was built, either 1810 or 1818. It ceased operation as a tollhouse in 1914 and has been used as a tavern, a residence, and now, museum.

All manner of people passed through this area of Franklin County. Indians, European settlers, frontiersmen, soldiers from numerous wars, merchants, laborers, and farmers all traveled on the road by the Toll House. Centuries overlap in layers of energy embedded in its thick, sturdy walls. Entities pausing there have revealed themselves to few, but they tell of a rough history and survival on what was once considered the western edge of civilization.

**Toll House #2 in the 1800s.**
*Courtesy and © of Michael J. Albert.*

# Apparitions

## The First Floor

The overwhelming feeling that dominates the first floor of the Toll House, a whisper away from the paved highway that is now Route 30, is that of people sitting at long tables, eating and drinking. It is likely that this portion of the Toll House was used as a tavern at one time. Candles are on the tables and the air is hazy with smoke. The room is crowded with people. In the still of the night, the conversations and exchanges between the people in the room is experienced as a low, rolling rumble heard between the sounds of vehicles passing on the busy highway.

Toward the back of the house, the atmosphere in the candlelit kitchen area is rambunctious. Men are coming and going through the side door to get something to drink. All of them are holding mugs. Most are smoking clay pipes. The air is thick with their pipe smoke and the smells of the kitchen. Their loud banter is punctuated by laughter. Although wars have been fought in the area, this is a time between wars. The men are from all walks of life and some even speak different languages, but there is no hostility in the room.

They are dressed in various types of clothing, neither fancy nor distinguished with the exception of one gentleman smoking a long, white pipe, leaning up against the side of the fireplace. His striking, colorful clothes and self-assured manner dominates the room. Some of the men stare at him, others laugh at him, and a quiet few respect him. He is dressed in the uniform of a Zouave.

The original Zouaves were members of the Zouaoua tribe from the hills of Algeria who volunteered to serve in the French Army in the early 1830s. They brought with them their distinctive uniforms and reputation as fierce fighters. The French military adopted their mode of dress and created elite Zouave fighting units that saw action in North Africa, the Crimea, and Italy in the 1850s.

In the United States, some city militias had already adopted the colorful uniform prior to the Civil War. The distinctive uniforms consisted of a fez with a brightly colored tassel, a turban, a vest, a tight-fitting short jacket, wide sash or belt, baggy pantaloons, and leggings. The jackets and vests were elaborately decorated with brass buttons and brightly colored trim or braid.

Numerous Zouave regiments, distinguished by their uniforms, were organized from Union troops while the Confederates fielded only a few. Two Zouave regiments that saw extensive action during the Civil War were the 5th New York Volunteer Infantry, known as "Duryee's Zouaves" after its first colonel, Abram Duryee, and the Philadelphia Fire Zouaves, part of the 72nd Pennsylvania Volunteer Infantry, made up of firemen from Philadelphia.

The fellow leaning so confidently against the fireplace might be from one of these units, as both saw action in this part of the country. He might be one of the hundreds mustered out after the war and on his way home or to parts unknown.

His clothing is made of wool and is grey in color. His blousy pants are tight at the waist and billow downward without shape; tucked into his high boots, the material flows over his shins like a balloon. His pants are held in place by a wide brown leather belt with a metal buckle. His short grey jacket is trimmed with thick red piping on the sleeves and along the edges. The jacket has an open, stand-up collar with no lapels; red piping outlines the collar. The jacket barely covers his flimsy white linen shirt. The shirt is laced with long strings that tie at the neck. He is wearing a red fez.

He has light brown hair and a fair complexion. The only hair on his thin face is a tiny moustache.

His voice is polished and eloquent and almost British in its affect. No one else in the room acts like him, looks like him, or speaks like him. He is totally different and he totally stands out—and he likes that.

It's clear that he is not here to stay. He is headed west. Whatever conflict he was involved in has been over for some time. He is moving on to an uncertain future.

### The Second Floor

Two men started a fight downstairs in the kitchen. They both had been drinking and were, in fact, friends. From their clothing it appears they might have been laborers or dockworkers from the mid to late 1800s. They wear dark, shapeless pants, light shirts with short leather vests, and one has tied a red scarf around his neck. What began as a lighthearted discussion deteriorated into a drunken brawl that threatened to have them both thrown out. The more sober of the two friends went upstairs to get away, but the other followed.

Their argument continues and they begin to throw punches. Then one takes out a small knife and stabs the other in the chest. It's not a big knife and, although it stings terribly, the wound will not kill him. He stumbles down the stairs to get help while his former friend flees.

Gettysburg monument honoring the 72nd Pennsylvania Volunteer Infantry Philadelphia Fire Zouaves.

**Toll House #2**

# Epilogue

Toll House #2 exists today because of all the events set forth in this story. Absent any one of the many elements that combined to ensure its survival, the Toll House would have disappeared from the earth.

What began with the birth of "Mad" Anthony Wayne in a timeline that includes the War for Independence, the Treaty of Greenville, the Civil War, the establishment of the National Road, the invention of the automobile, and the acquisition of Toll House #2 by the Franklin County Historical Society-Kittochtinny will eventually result in the establishment of the St. Thomas Historical Society and Museum in a formerly much visited and currently much haunted place.

Until then, the sounds and the smells of the souls who passed through the doors of Toll House #2 over the decades will continue unnoticed in the empty house. There will be eating and drinking in the front room and drinking and smoking in the back. The apparition by the fireplace will continue to savor his pipe and revel in his own presence while, in another era, two men will yell and fight upstairs in an endless replay of a long ago row.

It remains to be seen how the space will be shared when new residents join the crowded past.

Toll House #2.

# 11

## The Capitol Theatre

**159 South Main Street,**
**Chambersburg, Pennsylvania**

Owned and operated by the Pottstown Theater Company, the Capitol Theatre, located on South Main Street in Chambersburg, opened February 3, 1927. The theater, which at one time hosted traveling vaudeville acts and silent movies, featured a Moller Pipe Organ, something that no other theater in the area had at the time. Later "talkies" and musicals drew patrons from all over Franklin County. Air conditioning was added in 1955, but by then the Capitol Theatre, having gone through several owners, was in decline. The Greater Chambersburg Chamber of Commerce purchased the theater in 1996 with a grant from the Wood Foundation of Chambersburg. After a decade of repair, restoration, and rehabilitation, the Capitol Theatre is now a vibrant cultural arts center featuring stage acts and performances, as well as classic films utilizing a state-of-the-art digital projector and audio system.

## Wilford

Wilford Binder of Baltimore specified the requirements for the Moller Organ, produced by the eminent manufacturer in Hagerstown,

**The Capitol Theatre, Chambersburg.**

Maryland, that was installed in the theater in the 1930s. Wilford was the organ's main operator until 1952. He lived in an apartment on the second floor of the theater (now the ballet studio) and, in addition to playing the organ, served as the theater's manager, projectionist, and overall caretaker. He died in the Capitol Theatre and is believed to have never left.

Employees, technicians, and guests have complained of feeling a presence in the aisles and in the seats, both on the main floor and in the balcony. "It's as if someone just walks up next to you and is standing there, watching what you're doing," explained Randy, a member of the theater's staff. He and others have felt an unseen hand brush the back of their necks or touch them slightly on the back while walking down the aisle in various parts of the seating area. They have always assumed it's Wilford.

"He's a friendly ghost," Randy commented. "He likes to play practical jokes on people."

According to Randy, Wilford usually acts up when a full house is present in the theater or just before a huge crowd is expected. Sprinkler system head covers high up in the ceiling will somehow untwist themselves and fall off. Lights will go on and off, and audio systems will not work without coaxing.

One memorable incident occurred when, just before a performance, none of the microphones would work. Randy checked the entire system over and over again and found nothing amiss. He then walked up to one of the microphones on stage and said, "All right, Wilford, just give us some sound." Randy glimpsed a sprinkler cover fall to the floor from the ceiling above as the sound system suddenly came on.

**Interior of the Capitol Theatre.**

Although any unexplained events in the theater are attributed to Wilford, it cannot be ascertained with certainty that the entity moving about the aisles, balcony, and all areas of the theater is indeed Wilford Binder. At any rate, this entity is not alone.

## *Apparitions*

### The Stage

The stage is the domain of at least one entity commanding the back right corner facing out at the audience. He's dressed in a cowboy outfit: hat, blue denim shirt, vest, calico scarf, wide belt with an exaggerated belt buckle, very worn boots, wrangler pants, and leather chaps. Spurs on his boots jingle constantly. He is wiry and thin with sandy brown hair and a thick, bushy moustache.

He is portraying a rough character who provides comic relief during serious scenes by uttering lines that elicit waves of laughter from the audience.

Music plays and he is singing—shouting, actually—the words. At times he jumps around, dancing, kicking his legs up high, and flapping his arms.

He is all by himself and stays in the corner, and he is having a great time.

### The Catwalk

The original catwalk from 1927 is still in place and so is a backstage worker who remains there, at his post, raising and lowering the curtain and

View from the stage of the Capitol Theatre.

backdrops. He is far above the stage and doesn't have a problem being up there at all. He maneuvers around the numerous ropes, some of which are attached to sandbags, and knows his way around so well he doesn't even bother turning on lights.

He might be Irish. He has a tiny thin moustache, dark hair, and is small in stature. He is wearing a herringbone cap and a white shirt with rolled-up sleeves. The linen shirt has a stand-up collar and three or four buttons at the neck. He is wearing brown pants made out of cotton twill.

This is *his* area and he is very happy. He does not leave the catwalk and he likes being alone.

### The Child

A mischievous child, five or six years old, with sparkly blue eyes, long strawberry blonde hair, and a ruddy complexion runs around the back of the stage, peeking out at the audience between the scenery. The child has an androgynous face, so it's difficult to ascertain if it is a boy or a girl. The energy is that of a boy, but the entity resembles a girl from the early 1900s. It's wearing something blue and pointed buttonhole boots. The child is constantly laughing and is fascinated with the audience. This entity has some connection with whomever is in the projection booth.

### The Organ

Sitting at the Moller Organ in the front of the theater is a woman wearing a lacy white dress from the 1930s. The sleeves are puffed at the shoulders and gathered at the elbows. The dress has a stand-up collar lined in lace, and there is lace around the forearms. The back of the dress fans out slightly, like a small bustle. Her brown hair is flecked with red. Pulled back into a bun, some stray strands fall down around the sides of her face and this annoys her, as she is incredibly fastidious.

**Interior of the Capitol Theatre.**

The pages of her music must be turned at exactly the right time. She sits at the organ with perfect posture; her rigid, straight back facing the audience that watches the silent movies projected above her on the screen.

She is in her 20s and is a music teacher. Her name might be Sarah or Jane. She plays the organ here in the theater as a second job because she needs the money to support her family. A flu epidemic or other contagion that struck the community killed her father, and her mother suffers from some sort of physical impairment. Her only desire was to teach music, to give lessons,

**Projector, Capitol Theatre.**

but her life did not work out the way she intended and she is a little resentful.

### Wilford?

Another entity follows people throughout the theater. Sometimes it brushes the back of their necks; sometimes it stands beside or behind them. It is felt in the aisles and seats on the first floor, in the lobby, on the stage, and even in the basement. Sometimes it ventures into the projection booth. Its favorite vantage point is in the balcony, where it can watch over its domain and see everything that is going on.

This entity may or may not be energy remaining from Wilford Binder, but it's likely that this is the entity responsible for the unexplained happenings attributed to Wilford.

He watches over the theater, making sure that all is well. He would likely fix things that are malfunctioning or leave clues as to what needs to be repaired. He would never break anything.

He lets people know he is there because he likes to be in control. This is *his* theater.

But all is not peaceable in this unearthly kingdom. Tension exists between this entity and another energy, which is not present in the theater but permeates it. It is negative energy from someone with a great deal of money who believes the theater should be run a certain way and does not like change. This is a wealthy person; a moneyman who has contributed funds to the theater or holds a position that controls the theater.

The conflict between the energy of this rich and powerful man and the Wilford entity is palpable. Wilford remains so that the moneyman does not have his way.

## Epilogue

Theaters are generally prime locations for hauntings due to the variety and intensity of the emotional energy expended by actors, stage workers, employees, and the audience. Evidence indicates the Capitol Theatre is no exception, hosting residual and traditional energies. The next time you see a show or movie at the Capitol Theatre and feel someone sitting beside you in an empty seat or catch a glimpse of a dancing cowboy in the corner of the stage, don't doubt your eyes or senses. Just sit back, relax, and enjoy the show.

# 12

# Renfrew Museum & Park

**1010 East Main Street, Waynesboro, Pennsylvania**

## The Nicodemuses

E dward A. Miller answered the telephone on the first ring. It was 2 a.m. on the morning of July 7, 1973. He knew who would be on the other end of the line even before he answered.

Emma Geiser Nicodemus, widow of Edgar A. Nicodemus, had been in declining health for some time. Nurses had been providing twenty-four-hour in-home care for the eighty-one-year old Emma, enabling her to remain in her home, which was what she had wanted more than anything.

The stone house she lived in had been built in 1812 by Daniel Royer and had remained in the Royer family until the 1890s when Dr. A. H. Strickler purchased it. The John H. Minnich family worked the farm as tenants during Strickler's ownership and left in 1933. Mr. and Mrs. Clarence Beaver then occupied the Royer House until 1942 when Edgar Nicodemus, a wealthy orchardist and businessman, purchased it.

"Mrs. Nicodemus wants you to come over right away," the night nurse told him.

Edward, living with his wife in a nearby house on the Nicodemus property, was there in minutes.

Pioneers in the fruit tree business in the late 1800s, the Nicodemus family established orchards stretching across portions of Washington County, Maryland and Franklin County, Pennsylvania. Edward's father had worked for the Nicodemuses as far back as 1918, managing aspects of their orchard and cold storage business. Edward himself began to work for them in the 1940s taking care of the more than one hundred-acre property. In 1952, Edward was offered the house on the Nicodemus property in Waynesboro and a position with the Nicodemus family business that eventually evolved into a lifetime association.

Edward sat down beside Emma's bed and leaned close, letting her know he was there. "I'm so glad you're here," Emma said to him. "Call my doctor… Call my doctor…" These would be her last words.

Twelve hours later, Emma Geiser Nicodemus was dead.

## Footsteps

Emma had bequeathed the main house, the barn, and numerous historic structures occupying the 107 acres of her estate to the borough of Waynesboro to be converted into a museum and park, but this would not happen for months and there was an immediate need to secure the property.

The Royer House, filled with antiques and Early American decorative artifacts, had no security system, and there was concern that the stately home and its valuable contents would be a target for thieves once Emma's death was made public. Edward was asked if he would stay in the house at night until an appropriate security system could be installed. Edward agreed, with his wife joining him at night in the historic home. They stayed in one of the guest rooms on the second floor.

It began the first night.

Edward and his wife were lying in bed when they heard footsteps downstairs on the main floor. They listened as the footsteps came up the steps and stopped. Edward got out of bed and checked to see if someone had entered the house. Nothing had been disturbed and there was no one there.

This happened every night.

"We would be lying in bed, perfectly still, perfectly quiet," Edward said, and then they would hear footsteps coming up the steps. "[Most] nights, I didn't move, I would just listen." But the sound clearly upset his wife and, on nights when she couldn't stand it anymore, she told him, "You've got to get up and see who's in this house!"

Edward never discovered a source for the footsteps.

After two weeks, his wife announced, "I don't know about you, Ed, but I'm not staying here one more night."

# The Renfrew Sisters

Sisters Sarah and Jane Renfrew, for whom the museum and park in Waynesboro are named, may in fact have never existed, and legends describing their bloody deaths at a time when the area known as Franklin County was the western edge of the American frontier cast disturbing shadows across grounds that today are stunningly beautiful and calm. While some elements of the tales differ, the main allegations are consistent and contain all the inflammatory prejudices decorating stories born from history's regrets.

No date is recorded; however, it is supposed that the murder of the Renfrew sisters occurred near or during the Revolutionary War and represented one of the last massacres committed by Indians in Franklin County. Other accounts claim the girls were murdered during the last raid of Pontiac's War in 1764.

The Renfrew sisters, ten-year old Sarah and twelve-year old Jane, allegedly resided in a log house situated along the banks of the East Branch of the Antietam Creek, near a grist mill known to have been on the property later owned by A. J. Fahnestock, grandson of Daniel Royer. Depending on the account cited, the girls were washing clothes, either in a tub by their house or along the banks of the Antietam, or they were on horseback when two Indians descended them upon.

The Indians murdered the two sisters. Different versions have the girls being shot or bludgeoned to death. All accounts are consistent, however, in asserting that Sarah and Jane were scalped, with their killers taking their scalps.

Superstition held that a victim whose scalp had been torn away would not rest in death until the scalp was returned and buried with the body. Those who found the bodies of the murdered girls therefore believed it imperative that the scalps be recovered or the girls' souls would never find peace.

Two experienced hunters tracked the Indians across the countryside. Some more detailed accounts call these hunters the "Brothers Harn." Other tales assert that one of the hunters had, at one time, lived with Indians. Whoever they were, it took them two days to track the Indians to a "cove" in the Tuscarora Mountains near Mercersburg, Pennsylvania. The Indians were resting, eating plums.

It's on these points that all of the stories agree: the hunters, undetected, crept closer and closer to their quarry. They held their fire until they could actually see the plum pits fall from the Indians' mouths. Then they shot and killed them.

The hunters retrieved the scalps of the Renfrew sisters and returned with them, along with the scalps of the two Indians, in time for the sisters' burial. The only problem was that the girls' scalps had already been looped, which was a way of tying the scalps to dry them, resulting in the loss of some of the tissue. All four scalps were laid down upon the girls' coffins and placed in the graves with them.

Tradition has it that the sisters were buried in what was the Burns family graveyard on the Fahnestock property. The bodies were allegedly moved to the Covenanter Cemetery, now contained within the parameters of Renfrew Park, sometime in the 1830s. A slab of sandstone bearing no identification marked their graves.

These graves have never been found.

Over the years, visitors to the park who have found themselves on the grounds at dusk have claimed to have seen two young girls off in the distance, back beyond the Fahnestock house, wandering along the banks of the Antietam. Upon closer inspection, some claim to have seen blood pouring down from their heads where their hair should have been. They are, it is claimed, searching for the missing parts of their scalps.

## *The Royer House*

The Royer House at Renfrew Museum and Park is the centerpiece of the park. Thousands tour the house every year. Classes for children and lectures for adults are regularly offered in the main rooms of the house, covering topics both educational and recreational. Hundreds of visitors come to see the candlelit Christmas Open House in December each year.

But children attending workshops and other events have complained of being watched by an indefinable presence in the corner of the open-hearth kitchen on the main floor and have fidgeted uneasily during lectures in the adjacent dining room. Some have fled the basement, where the restroom is located, suddenly, without reason, unable to identify what frightened them and refusing to return no matter what.

Employees of the museum and park had always assumed that should any energy remain in the old house, it would likely be that of the Nicodemuses. Dinner parties, sporting events, and legendary hospitality defined their years there and it was assumed that Edgar or Emma might linger, filling the house with their warmth and welcome. But this does not appear to be so. The energy that permeates the Royer House and dominates every past existence is neither warm nor welcoming.

## *Apparitions*

### The Man with the Scythe

It cannot be said with certainty that the man seen holding the scythe in the kitchen of the Royer House at Renfrew is Daniel Royer,

nor can it be asserted beyond doubt that the woman cowering near him is his wife. But the names of two of Royer's children, daughters Polly and Susan, have been heard there, and a disembodied voice has whispered, "Susan was beaten in the basement."

The man in the kitchen stands around five feet six or seven inches tall. A long, thin grey beard frames his gaunt face with sandy-colored whiskers along the edges. His bald crown is encircled by thinning, sandy hair. His skin has a yellow tinge to it and he doesn't appear to be well.

His pants are high-waisted and light-colored, made of linen material identical to that used in feed sacks of the time. His beard hides the top of his pants so that suspenders or straps cannot be seen. His shirt is white with tiny blue stripes running vertically through the material every four to five inches. He is holding a scythe in one hand and gestures with the other as he walks back and forth in the area in front of the pantry.

His family listens to him because they and everyone who knows him are afraid of him.

His wife stands near him, but does not speak. Her graying light brown hair has a reddish hue to it. It is pulled back, away from her face. She is wearing a pinafore over her dress, like an apron. Her cotton dress displays a check-like pattern colored by bits of maroon and pine green on an off-white background.

**Royer House, Renfrew Museum and Park, Waynesboro.**

The pinafore is the same color as her husband's pants and looks as if it were made from the same linen-like material. Her dress is perfectly starched, but the pinafore over it is wrinkled.

She is very thin and, while her complexion is not jaundiced, it is not that of a healthy being.

The source of their illness is the water. Something is wrong with the water.

*(It is known that Daniel Royer, one of the more prosperous of the Pennsylvania German farmers who settled in and around Waynesboro, ran a tannery on the property and a grist mill, both of which required water. One or both of these operations could have contaminated the drinking water.)*

The personality emanating from the male apparition is stern and intolerant. He is known for his temper and no one wants to cross him. He holds a position in the community where his opinions of people matters and, for this reason as well, people wanted to stay on his "good" side. But this was very hard to do.

And while no one ever saw him beat his wife, he gave the impression he would not hesitate to beat anyone who crossed him.

He does not stay in the kitchen, although that is where his presence is most strongly felt.

He is also felt in a room toward the back of the house known as the rear parlor. Visitors sensitive to such impressions have commented that this room "feels like money." *(Daniel Royer was a state legislator and local tax collector and this room served as his office. Residents came to his house to pay their taxes, entering and exiting through an adjacent door.)*

No matter where one walks in the Royer House, it seems as if this male entity is following. He is clearly not happy about you being there. He is clearly not happy about anything.

## The Second Floor Bedroom

Someone died in agony in the bedroom known as the northwest chamber, on the second floor of the Royer House. He is a young man, perhaps between seventeen and nineteen years of age, and does not appear to be related in time to the apparitions occupying the first floor.

He is burning up with fever and is flailing about on the bed, back and forth, flipping from side to side, delirious. His dark hair is plastered to his head by sweat and his soaked white shirt clings to his thin body.

His moans and cries fill the air. There is no one there to care for him.

He does not have a connection to the rest of the house and might be a tenant or migrant worker who resided there temporarily when the house had no permanent occupants. His energy attached itself to this room because this is where he suffered and died.

Something on the property caused this illness.

Something is wrong with the water.

## The Basement

An uneasy feeling greets visitors to the basement. The air in the window bays along the back of the house is thin and tense. Skin tingles and the heart races. It feels like fear.

People waited there, frightened, nervous, anticipating pain. They were not slaves or servants. They were the children of the owners—sent there by their mother.

When they had disobeyed or had in some other way incurred the displeasure of one or both parents, their mother would tell them to wait in the basement for their father. Their father would let them wait there for hours in terrified anticipation of the punishment to come. Then he would come down the basement stairs and beat them, using leather straps that were hanging there for this very purpose.

A visitor has heard, "Susan was beaten in the basement." The voice had been clear and distinct. It came from the air. Others have discerned soft, faint cries and slapping sounds, but rarely has anyone heard the voice. The name "Polly" has been heard in the kitchen.

Royer and his wife, Catherine, had ten children, four boys and six girls. Susan and Polly were two of their daughters.

## The Underground Railroad

The back windows of the Royer House sometimes flicker with candlelight from phantom sources as shadows move northward along the Antietam Creek, barely discernable within the unmoving trees. Many people are following the creek. They are dark-skinned. Light-skinned people move among them with torches, guiding their movement, encouraging, quietly hurrying them along. Candles in the windows signal that all is clear.

Few have glimpsed these lights. Most have assumed any lights seen in the windows at night are the reflections of headlights passing by on Main Street.

No streets, however, pass behind the house. And the shadows seen moving along the creek at night have always been dismissed as imaginary.

The East Branch of the Antietam Creek flows by the Royer house and through the grounds of Renfrew Park. Trees along the banks of the creek provide cover to anyone following the water. Impressions suggest the Antietam served as a passageway on the Underground Railroad. Visions of people moving along the creek are identical to those seen along the Antietam several miles south of Renfrew Park, where the East Branch flows near Lyons Road.

# Epilogue

Renfrew Park is open all year from dawn to dusk and features picnic tables, grills, a playground, miles of walking and hiking trails, open fields, shade trees, and masses of flowers in the spring. In addition to the Royer House, several historic structures occupy the restored 1830s-era farmstead. Although most of the stories contained in the structures and grounds of Renfrew have yet to be revealed, it is clear that more than antique furniture and artistic artifacts occupy the Royer House.

The next time you visit the Royer House, be aware that you might be crossing paths with an acrimonious male entity resentful of your presence. He cannot hurt you, as he did his children, but you might feel his breath as he leans near you, urging you to leave.

You might hear the last, sorrowful gasps of a young man who passed away alone in the bedroom upstairs. You might hear footsteps or whispers. If you need to use the restroom, be prepared for what might await you in the basement.

Should you pass by the park at night, glance toward the Royer House and ascertain if candles beckon in the windows, signaling escaped slaves that the night is safe for passage. And don't be startled if your headlights catch the silhouettes of two young girls walking through the grounds long after the park has closed, something dark and moist dripping from their heads.

**Rear of the Royer House, Renfrew Museum and Park.**

# 13

# The John Brown House

**225 East King Street, Chambersburg, Pennsylvania**

## The Meeting

**H**ad there been surveillance cameras and tracking devices in existence in August 1859, they would have recorded a meeting of alleged domestic terrorists at an abandoned quarry on the outskirts of Chambersburg. Microphones previously secreted in the fishing gear carried as a ruse by one of the subjects would have transmitted their conversation to government agents. What would have been discovered was that the main subject, John Brown, using the alias Dr. Isaac Smith, was planning a raid on a federal arsenal in Harpers Ferry, in what is now West Virginia, and was soliciting the assistance of the most well-known African American leader of the time, Frederick Douglass.

Chambersburg was probably selected by Brown as the main location from which to plan the Harpers Ferry raid because it was the hub of the Cumberland Valley Railroad and provided easy transportation for people and supplies throughout Pennsylvania and neighboring states. From June through October of that fateful year, John Brown rented a room at 225 East King Street, a Chambersburg boarding house owned by Mary Ritner. Ritner's father-in-law, Joseph Ritner, had served as the governor of Pennsylvania from 1835 to 1839 and had been an outspoken opponent of slavery. It's likely that

Brown sought residence there on purpose, given the anti-slavery sympathies of the Ritner family. Although known by appearance, Brown identified himself as Dr. Isaac Smith and claimed to be an iron mine developer. He was joined at the boarding house at various times by John Henry Kagi and other members of his "army" as they sought supplies and planned their fateful raid.

On August 19, 1859, Brown and Kagi met with Douglass and Shields Green, a fugitive slave from Charleston, South Carolina, at the quarry in Chambersburg. Brown, fifty-nine years old, was a hunted man at this time, wanted by authorities for ordering the execution-style murders of pro-slavery men along the Pottawatomie Creek in Kansas. In meetings that lasted almost two days, Brown tried to convince Douglass his raid on Harpers Ferry would succeed and sought his endorsement. But Douglass was certain the raid would fail and would in fact cause more harm to the anti-slavery movement than good if he encouraged African Americans to follow Brown. Neither succeeded in convincing the other of his position, but they parted friends. Douglass traveled to Rochester, New York, while Brown stayed in Chambersburg and proceeded with his plans for the raid on Harpers Ferry. Shields Green chose to go with Brown.

On October 16, 1859, Brown and his "army" of twenty-one men attacked and seized the federal arsenal at Harpers Ferry. Within thirty-six hours, however, most of Brown's men had been captured or killed. Brown himself was wounded and upon his arrest was imprisoned in Charlestown, West Virginia. He was tried and convicted of treason on November 2 and was hanged December 2, 1859.

~~~~~~~

In the years just prior to the house's purchase by the Kittochtinny Historical Society, it served as an office building for the American Heart Association and the March of Dimes. Those whose offices occupied the first floor experienced a bitter chill when walking across certain areas of the house. These experiences were most common in the front parlor next to the street, a room dominated by a large fireplace. The sounds of footsteps made by unseen tenants on the floors and the main stairway were common, but no one ever became accustomed to them. People whose offices occupied the second floor frequently looked up in anticipation of someone coming up the stairs...only to see no one arrive. At night, the fear increased, as the sense of being watched or the breeze of a phantom touch became magnified by shadows. And the same disquieting footsteps heard during the day somehow always seemed louder and more menacing in the dark.

Built in the 1830s, the house at 225 East King Street has seen generations of families and scores of tenants within its walls. There is no doubt the energy of some of these souls remains; however, it's not unexpected that the strongest presence is that of John Brown. While it can never be said for certain it is his essence that dominates, his appearance, as recorded by old photographs, and his manner, as described by contemporaneous writers, give credence to the belief

that some of Brown's energy remains very much a part of Mary Ritner's boarding house.

## *Apparitions*

Those who have seen him claim he is John Brown, recognizing him from known photographs and descriptions. Those who have not seen him have *felt* him, in sudden chills and faint touches. When he is present, an uneasy tension prickles the skin and the air is charged, as if a small tornado is tearing through the house. The energy is turbulent.

He is sitting in the front room, in a Windsor chair in front of the fireplace, his back toward the fire and the light. There is no other light and he is alone. It's as if he doesn't want anyone to see him there...he doesn't want anyone to ever know his movements. Not ever. He never lights candles, choosing instead to move by instinct in the dark.

His long legs are splayed out in front of the chair and his long arms rest limply down at his sides. There is a zealous gleam in his silvery-grey eyes, barely visible in the shadows of his face. His hair and beard are wild and unkempt. He has not bathed with any regularity. He has not eaten for days and has taken only water. Those who accompany him are aware of these emotional states that seize him from time to time. The episodes generally last seven to ten days and are followed by a mellow time in which he can once again deal with the world. But during these spells he is obsessive and can't even quiet his mind long enough to sleep.

Resting near one leg of the chair, on the floor, is a journal. It is small, approximately six or seven inches in length and a few inches wide. It has a soft, leathery binder with no writing on it, and the pages inside are solid white. It is flexible and easily hidden. Right now, at this moment, he is obsessed with the small book and what he has written in it.

**The John Brown House, Chambersburg.**

He believes he is the "word and the way" and he is above and beyond the world around him. God speaks to him directly and he alone knows what must be done. He is a savior of people and he is not afraid because God will watch out for him. Manic and calm at the same time, he raises his hands in prayer and looks into the darkness.

His square face with its hard features is in silhouette against the blazing fire behind him.

Eventually he will rise and walk across the room to the staircase. Bending slightly at the doorway so as to get his tall frame through without banging his head, he will then slowly ascend the stairs to his bedroom. There he will lie for hours in the dark, praying and planning.

Another presence resides in the house...one that is cognizant of the danger he is in and fears the windows. He might or might not be associated with John Brown. Some believe he resembles Brown's co-conspirator, Kagi. Workers have glimpsed him as a shadow in the side of the eye, dissolving quickly upon full glance. He hides in the corner of the room adjacent to the parlor, and watches and listens for people outside the windows, along the side of the house. He knows people are looking for him. It is night and, from his position, he can hear people approach and watch those who pass in the alley. He can see if they look in the windows. He is wearing grey clothing, making him less visible in the dark, as he stands plastered up against the wall in the corner, facing the windows.

**Front room of the John Brown House—the apparition of John Brown has been seen sitting in front of the fireplace.**

He is portly and short. His head is very round and his fine, thinning hair has a curl or wave to it. He has tight, shiny skin, a ruddy complexion, and his full face is framed by mutton-chop sideburns. His short neck is almost one with his huge belly.

He knows that if he is discovered he will be killed. His fear adds to the unsettling atmosphere of the house.

Outside the house, in the alley, three men skulk around the windows, trying to pry inside without being seen. They wear what

appear to be dark green riding britches and high, laced field boots. They are hunters of some sort and they are not from this area. They have followed someone here. They sneak up and down the alley, crouched low, and raise their heads to look quickly inside the windows. This is what they do and this is where they stay.

Neighbors have heard their footsteps.

# Epilogue

The John Brown House, as it is known today, was renovated and opened as a museum in the spring of 2009, housing antique furniture, artifacts, documents, and photographs pertaining to the life and death of John Brown and chronicling his time in Chambersburg prior to the raid on Harpers Ferry.

No matter who eventually comes to occupy the house or what use the house will have, the John Brown entity will continue to sit in front of the fireplace, facing away, consumed by his religious fervor and the journal containing his thoughts. He will eventually rise, bend at the doorway, and walk up the stairs to his bedroom...his phantom footsteps confusing anyone who might be there to hear.

A presence will still stand in the corner, watching from the dark, frightened by the windows. If someone should lean against the wall there in just the right place, they might feel the chill of fear.

And although probably unnoticed by visitors, disembodied footsteps will still scurry along the alley by the windows. People outside might hear it, but the museum will be closed and no one will be there to see the face perpetually peering through the window at night.

**Fireplace in the front room of the John Brown House.**

# 14

# The Underground Railroad

Franklin County, because of its location on the Maryland border just north of the Mason-Dixon Line, evolved into a major artery of the Underground Railroad during the early 1800s and continued as such up until the Civil War. The Underground Railroad refers to the numerous routes, hiding places or "safe houses," different modes of transportation, participants, and supporters of the effort to facilitate the escape of slaves from southern states to the northern states and Canada. Following the end of the Revolutionary War, organized groups in various parts of the country began to offer assistance to runaway slaves. Individual communities operating in different parts of the country eventually developed an organized system to move slaves to freedom. This system came to be called the "Underground Railroad" sometime during the early 1830s, borrowing its nomenclature from the emerging steam railroads that were being built across the country.

In addition to adopting the railroad metaphor, participants used railroad terminology to describe elements of the process. Routes of escape were known as "lines." These routes typically led from one "safe house" to another and were locations where fugitive slaves were hidden until they could be moved again. "Stations" were stopping places, "conductors" were the people assisting in the escape, and "freight" was the name given to the slaves themselves.

The passage of the Fugitive Slave Act of 1850, which mandated the arrest of any actual or suspected escaped slave anywhere in the United States, resulted in an increase in the number of slaves fleeing the United States for Canada. This naturally caused a dramatic increase in the number of "passengers" and in the number of people dedicated to assisting them all along the various lines of the Underground Railroad.

## *Apparitions*

### The East Branch of the Antietam Creek

The East Branch of the Antietam Creek meanders through Waynesboro, Pennsylvania, just three miles north of the Mason-Dixon Line, and continues its southwesterly flow into Maryland. From the founding of Franklin County until well after the Civil War, few houses stood near its route and the banks of the creek were typically rocky and shaded by forest. The isolation of the waterway and its convenient passage from Maryland to Pennsylvania and to further points north made it an ideal "line" for the Underground Railroad.

As with many aspects of the Underground Railroad, historical documentation confirming routes through Franklin County is still sketchy, but evidence of "safe houses" in the county, recorded recollections by escaped slaves and "conductors" support a valid assumption that the East Branch of the Antietam was indeed a major passageway north—the intense energy associated with this effort, the fear, the desperation, and the hope has apparently embedded itself in its banks.

A stunning consistency to the apparitions appearing along the creek bears witness to the trembling terror of those fleeing for freedom and the danger and risk to those who helped the escaping slaves. Shadows moving along the banks are led by phantom torches and signaled by flickering phantom candles in an endlessly repeated trek stretching for miles along the winding creek.

A large, majestic house commands a site above the Antietam Creek off Lyons Road in Washington Township. The house is accessed by a bridge across the creek bed and dates to the 1790s. When the property was originally surveyed in the 1750s, the Mason-Dixon Line had not yet been established and eventually some of the property belonging to the homestead came to be in the state of Maryland while the majority of the property remained in Pennsylvania. The house, barn, outbuildings, and farmlands surrounding them had been known as the "Antietam Home" farm during the mid-1800s, around the time Underground Railroad activity reached its zenith.

While the house has a peaceful feel to it, the basement—a series of large rooms and connecting tunnels—crackles with energy. Its thick, stone walls and dirt floors shelter numerous entities, all of whom appear to have been passengers on the Underground Railroad.

Throughout the years owners have reported hearing voices and footsteps in the basement. The sounds were not frightening and the feel was never malevolent. Sometimes the air would be stuffy, as if unseen people packed the seemingly unoccupied space. Other times nothing would be felt other than the damp and cool atmosphere of a stone walled basement.

Those sensitive to apparitions have seen black men and women huddled in the rooms and tunnels. They are not frightened. They are there with the blessing of the homeowners, waiting to move on. They are hiding in other areas of the house and property as well, but the largest group hides in the basement.

Mysterious lights have been seen in the attic; quick, bright flashes resembling sparklers that streak away as soon as they are spotted. This visual manifestation possibly pertains to the presence of two males who are apparently hiding in the attic. They roam the attic, but when someone approaches by way of the stairs, they flee to their hiding places in the corners of the room, flashes of light left by their energy. It isn't clear who these men are, but they are being hunted by authorities. They might have been "conductors" on the Underground Railroad who found sanctuary in the same house that served as a "station."

**The house on Lyons Road.**

At night from Lyons Road, some distance away on the other side of the creek, people driving by have sometimes seen dim, flickering light, like candlelight, coming from several of the windows on the second floor of the house. And along the creek they have seen shadows moving among the trees, guided in places by torches whose fleeting flames dissolve into darkness.

The very same apparitions have been seen at Renfrew Museum and Park, which shares the banks of the East Branch of the Antietam only a few miles north of the Lyons Road home.

## Rocky Spring Presbyterian Church

The Rocky Spring Presbyterian Church is located approximately four miles north of Chambersburg, on Rocky Spring Road, in Letterkenny Township. The congregation was organized in 1738 and the current brick building was constructed in 1794, replacing an earlier log structure. The church was built near the spring that bears its name and to this day remains in a comparatively remote, sparsely populated patch of Franklin County.

Currently administered by the Franklin County Chapter of the Daughters of the American Revolution, the church is associated with Revolutionary War history due to the actions of the Reverend John Creaghead, pastor of the church from 1768 to 1799. In July 1776, he inspired the entire male population of the congregation to fight in the war. They all departed and enlisted to fight in the cause for independence from Britain. Many are buried in the cemetery adjoining the church.

In the 1800s, the church came to be used only on Sundays for services and remained closed and deserted during the other six days and nights. This, coupled with its remote location alongside a spring, made it an ideal "station" on the Underground Railroad. The emotions of the people who found sanctuary there and the powerful personality of the pastor who protected them cause inexplicable temperature fluctuations and unexplained sounds in the isolated church, their residual energy venting in an endless replay that few have been present to see.

Impressions of escaped slaves huddled in the back pews of the church materialize from forces embedded in the church

**Rocky Spring Presbyterian Church.**

walls. It is night and the huddled wayfarers are waiting. There are men, women, and children and they are calm because they know they are safe in the church. Their energy can be felt when the air is still. Historians and restoration experts laboring in the church through the years have heard benches creak and groan along the back of the church, as if unseen entities were resting on the wood.

But the strongest presence in the silent church is the pastor who is felt there as well. He is the driving force behind hiding the

fugitives in the church and in helping the slaves to move north toward freedom. He would be described today as charismatic with a talent for getting people to follow him. In addition to those who assisted in Pennsylvania, he recruited and organized groups to participate in the Underground Railroad in Maryland and what was then western Virginia, particularly Morgantown.

He stands at the pulpit at the front of the church and stretches out his arms toward his congregation. With no excess bulk on his 5'6" frame, he moves in staccato fashion with short, sharp gestures and measured steps. His sermons are animated and theatrical. Everything he does—every movement, every thought, and every spoken word—is calculated. He knows what he is doing every minute of every day and has detailed plans for his future and for that of his congregation.

His name might be Jeremiah or, possibly, John. His expression is intense. The angular jaw of his clean-shaven face is set and firm and his dark, piercing eyes look right through you. His hair is very dark and cut at sharp angles in a blunt style, as if he might have trimmed it himself.

His charcoal pants are made from a twilled woolen cloth known as serge. He wears a white, long sleeved shirt with a tabbed collar open at the neck.

In addition to being the church's pastor, he owns a mill, quite possibility the one not far from the church on the Rocky Spring.

He is not married and there are no women in his life. Women are frivolous and he has no time for frivolities. The church, his mill, and the Underground Railroad consume him.

The ardor of this man, this reverend whose assertive personality and strength of conviction bent all who met him to his will,

**Interior, Rocky Spring Presbyterian Church.**

permeates the Rocky Spring Presbyterian Church. He watches over the people he has hidden there even as he plans to move others north to Canada, cajoling the community to believe as he does and enlisting their participation in his mission. He is tireless, intense, and determined, and his captivating sermons compel compliance.

To this day, on exceptional nights when the air is paused and empty, if you find yourself in the vicinity of the Rocky Spring Presbyterian Church, pay heed, because if you listen closely enough, you might actually hear his voice.

# 15

# The House in Chambersburg

## The Ornament

When Diane came down the stairs in the morning, the Christmas tree lights were lit and the ornament was on the floor again, several feet in front of the tree where it could not possibly have fallen, sitting facing the entrance, in the middle of the room. The barrister ornament...colorful and large, it looked like an old bewigged barrister from a Dickens novel.

The tree lights, the window lights, and the lights on the banister were all plugged in to the same timer. They were always off at night when she and her husband went to bed, but one or more of the lighted decorations were always on in the morning when one of them came down the stairs. And the barrister ornament was frequently on the floor.

She had moved the ornament several times, thinking that the branches she had placed it on had not been sturdy enough to support it. She gave up after placing the barrister on the back of the tree one night only to have it greet her in the morning again, on the floor, at the entrance to the room.

She had lived in the house with her husband Norman and their two sons for more than twenty-five years and all of them had grown accustomed to their unseen company. Every year the Christmas lights malfunctioned in some inexplicable manner, but this was the first time the ornaments had been fooled with. The barrister ornament was new.

Her sons were in their 20s now and one of them was an attorney... and whatever was in her house—*whether one or many*—clearly had a problem with lawyers.

# A Supernatural Welcome

The house had been built in 1805 when there was nothing on the east end of Chambersburg but fields and farms. Diane and Norman had always wanted a big house and this one had been affordable and livable. They moved in when their sons were young and over the years, the couple renovated, improved, and altered the house and the property. Today the magnificent house is surrounded by housing developments, the farms long having been sold and the fields paved over. Their sons went on to school and professions and moved not too far away, leaving Diane and Norman alone in the large house. But...they *weren't* really alone. In the original part of the house some previous occupants still remain.

The daughter of the previous owners had told them that "things went on" there. Their very first night in the house as a family, they all found out exactly what she had meant.

"All of the [metal] door latches started rattling at the same time," Diane recalled. She and her husband had just gone to bed and they sat up and looked at one another. They could hear latches jiggling downstairs, upstairs, everywhere. "We're not very scared people," Diane said. They decided that whatever it was, *it* was simply greeting them. "It was quite a sound. This has never happened again. Just the first night and that was it." The latches leaped as if to say, "We're here, we're here, we're sharing space with you."

In time they became accustomed to the paranormal phenomena.

Despite their efforts at climate control, the house seemed to have two temperature zones. The downstairs was always warm and inviting. The upstairs, no matter what the thermostat setting, was *always* cold, almost tense.

Small objects began to disappear. Diane would leave earrings on her dresser and they would be found on the kitchen counter.

Keys would vanish and reappear days later. Kitchen utensils would somehow find their way to the garage.

They would hear footsteps: light footsteps and heavy footsteps.

There was a piano in one of the rooms downstairs and often they would hear it ping as a key here and there played.

Sometimes lights would come on and go off. She would remember that she had turned a light on and would find it off. She would turn a light off and then find it on. Many times during the day, she would find lights on when there would have been no reason for anyone to turn them on.

They had a golden retriever, which would appear startled, and then stare and bark at empty rooms.

She would often see things out of the corner of her eye that might or might not have been there.

But it wasn't until her youngest son told her there were people in his room that she began to become concerned.

## *Angels*

There are three bedrooms on the second floor, one of which is the master bedroom. Their sons occupied the other two rooms. The youngest son had the first bedroom to the left at the top of the stairs. One afternoon when he was three years old, as Diane put him to bed for his nap, he asked her to close the bedroom door.

Other than when Diane and Norman watched television at night, the bedroom doors in their house were never closed.

"He asked me to close his bedroom door because he told me the people would talk to him only when his bedroom door was closed." Although this seemed unusual, Diane did not want to dwell on it for fear of emphasizing it. "He told me not to worry because they were good people, not bad." A short while later, her son told her he wanted to be an angel because the angels spoke to him.

He never described these "angels" other than to say that they were "beautiful." Diane stated, "He didn't really say if they were men or women. He never related conversations or what these people said to him. He [just] seemed very open to listening to what they had to say." He seemed to enjoy the presence of the "angels" and often repeated his desire to be one.

Again, Diane did not dwell on this or inquire further as she did not want her son to somehow fixate on whatever he believed was occurring.

The toddler continued to request that his door be closed at naptime. When he grew older and naps became a thing of the past, he stopped talking about the angels.

It would be some twenty years later before his mother found out about the closet doors.

## Closet Doors

Because her husband snores, many nights Diane sleeps in what had been their youngest son's bedroom. She recalled that the daughter of the previous owner had told her that when you slept in that room, you couldn't leave any part of your arms outside of the covers because "it" would touch you.

Diane had ignored that advice and had never felt anything touch her in that room until the night that something actually got into bed with her.

Diane was sleeping, but the movement of the covers and the bed woke her up. "It was really strange," she said. "The covers went back and the mattress went down," as if someone had gotten into bed beside her.

She didn't feel threatened or frightened. "When you've lived with it for so long, you get used to it." Diane simply rolled over and went back to sleep.

Her sons were at college at the time and when Diane spoke to them she told them what had happened. Both asked immediately, "Did you have the closet door locked?"

No, she told them. Why would she lock the closet door?

Her sons were born twenty-one months apart. As youngsters, they would take turns sleeping in each other's rooms. In the summer, one room was cooler so they slept in there. In the winter, the other room was warmer, so they slept there. Unbeknownst to their mother, they shared stories about their rooms.

"Well, you can't sleep in there if the closet door's not locked," her youngest son told her. Both sons declared, without details, that the closets are "evil" and that "bad things" happen when the closet doors are open. To this day when her sons are at home and sleep in their old rooms, they lock their closet doors.

Diane does not believe that there is anything "evil" in her house and the entity that crawled into bed with her meant her no harm. But not wanting to take any chances, she now keeps the closet doors locked.

## Raps and Jingles

Repeated raps came from their closed bedroom door and the latch and handle jumped and jingled. Diane and Norman were in bed watching television and had the door closed so as not to disturb the children. Diane got up and opened the door, but there was no one there. She walked over to her sons' bedrooms and found them fast asleep.

Diane got back into bed and not five minutes later..."*Rap, rap, rap, jingle, jingle, jingle.*" She got up, opened the door, and checked on her sons again. Nothing.

She closed their bedroom door and got back into bed and she and her husband watched the remaining minutes of the television show.

A short while later they turned off the television and Diane got up and opened the door to their bedroom. Just as she opened the door, "These footsteps raced down the center stairs." But there was no one and nothing there.

## Voices

Diane doesn't get the feeling that anyone follows her, but she sometimes hears things. She describes the sounds as, "Audible but not discernable." The sounds are always fairly near, right beside her. One night they woke her up.

Diane felt as if she had been sleeping for hours when in fact it had been only ten minutes. A voice called her name. She startled awake and looked over at her husband who was fast asleep beside her. Could he have been talking in his sleep? Diane waited, and then heard him snore. She turned over and fell back to sleep. Some moments later, she awoke again to her name being called. "When I woke up that time I looked out [the bedroom door] and saw the attic steps and there was this glowing, circular mass, wafting up the steps."

It was faint and circular, like a negative shadow, about the size of a basketball but not totally round. Diane wondered if it could have been headlights so she lay there a while, watching the patterns caused by the headlights of passing cars. No, that hadn't been it.

Whatever it was never came back and she never saw it again.

The sounds remain.

## The Family Room

They enclosed what had been a summer kitchen and turned it into a family room. A study accessed by steps was added above it on the second floor.

Norman would work in the study and call to Diane when he heard her walking around downstairs. He would hear items moving, footsteps, rustling.

His wife never answered because she was not there. Norman would come down and find Diane had been in another part of the house or outside.

Eventually they became accustomed to the sounds. Everything seemed to make noise, but nothing moved.

Their youngest son's girlfriend spent one night in the loft bedroom over the family room. In the morning she claimed she had not slept because she had heard footsteps and furniture moving and all kinds of sounds all night long. She has not returned to the house.

Their oldest son was visiting one Saturday night with his girlfriend. Diane and Norman had gone out and when they returned around 6:30 p.m., they found their guests "white as sheets."

Their son claimed that shortly after his parents left, the television began to malfunction. Then they heard an infant crying. They both heard the sobbing and wailing, but couldn't pinpoint where it was coming from. It went on for about twenty minutes—and it scared them.

A few days later a large wooden replica of the Seal of the United States prominently displayed in the family room lifted itself from its hook and flew off the wall.

## The Bathing Suit

They were going on vacation to Virginia Beach and Diane had purchased a matching sun hat to go with her favorite bathing suit. When she began to pack for the trip, she went to the drawer where she kept her bathing suits. Her favorite wasn't there.

She *knew* she had put it there, but it was gone. Diane tore the house apart looking for it. She couldn't find the bathing suit anywhere.

They were gone for three weeks and Diane was the first one in the house when they got back. She carried some items upstairs to the master bedroom. She gasped and dropped them on the floor when she walked through the door.

In the exact center of the bed, laying completely flat on the bedspread without a wrinkle in it, was her bathing suit.

## Destructive

Decorative plates are displayed on the plate rail along the kitchen wall. Diane watched one day as a plate actually moved four inches forward, fell off, and shattered on the counter. Over the years, numerous plates have fallen. "They just move out, then drop."

But it's what happened to the items in the attic that upsets her. It is the one destructive act by unseen hands that stays with her.

Her husband's grandmother had been an expert on the Inuit Indians and had worked in a museum when she was younger. She had given Diane some Inuit artifacts that Diane had placed in a paper bag along with some other items. There were some candles that had been carved to resemble totem poles, some items made out of sealskin, some ivory pieces, and some Inuit dolls. Also in the bag was an ivory stickpin one of her sons had made for her when he was six years old. Diane left the bag on the bottom steps to the attic, intending to put it away when she returned later in the day.

But when she got back that night, the bag had been ripped apart and most of the items were missing. When they looked around, they discovered that individual items from the bag had been placed in just about every room in the house.

The candles had been broken in as many as three places, the dolls were torn apart, and the ivory pieces smashed.

It would be weeks before Diane found the stickpin. Something had hidden it behind a lard can in the kitchen.

## Apparitions

While much residual energy permeates the house, two distinct traditional entities are suggested as accounting for the strongest activity.

On the first floor, in the room with the piano, there frequently stands a woman wearing a white dress with a dotted Swiss pattern and a small ruffle around the bottom.

She is standing by the piano, tinkering with the keys, absentmindedly playing a scale or a random note while looking out the window at her beloved garden. Her hair is dark in color and is worn up in a bun in back. Her bangs are curly with little ringlets along the sides of her face. She appears to be in her 30s and is getting that matronly-look about her.

She played the piano or an earlier version of the piano. She was very good. She would invite people in and she would play for them.

In her church, she played the organ and led the choir. Her husband did not approve. They were wealthy and of high standing in the congregation. She should have spent Sundays seated beside her husband in the front row of the church where people of their social stature belonged.

She spends most of her time in this room. She walks the original areas of the house and does not enter the additions and newer construction.

Her husband is there as well although he keeps his distance. The tension in the atmosphere on the second floor results from the animosity between the husband and the wife.

He was someone who controlled much money, possibly the president or chairman of the board of a bank, as he oversaw ledgers and books containing accounting information. He did not do the work himself; he delegated it.

He is short and somewhat stocky with bushy sideburns. He is dressed in an expensive dark suit indicative of his financial and social status.

A gruff person, he is generally disliked while his wife is much beloved. He resents the fact that his wife, while always passively resistant, now openly defies him, socially and privately. She has been this way since she lost their unborn child.

Someone, possibly their first child, was sick in the bedroom once occupied by Diane and Norman's youngest son and might have died there.

The wife was pregnant with their second child when she and her husband had a tragic altercation. She was attempting to escape from him by running up the stairs. When he grabbed her to pull her back, she fell down the flight of stairs. She ultimately lost their unborn child.

They slept in separate rooms. Sometimes he would bang on her door and attempt to force himself upon her. When she was away, his mistress comforted him.

He destroyed her personal belongings out of spite. She'd had a white, porcelain figure on top of her piano that she greatly treasured. He smashed it.

Today he seems to take his animosity out on the current mistress of the house while his wife takes refuge in the room with the piano.

# Epilogue

Unexplained occurrences are normal in this house.

The vacuum cleaner will sometimes just stop for no reason and then go on again. Diane has owned several vacuum cleaners and this has happened to all of them, in every room. She has had to tell housekeepers not to worry, that sometimes the vacuum cleaner will suddenly stop but will eventually turn on again.

The radios in her sons' former bedrooms turn off and on at will. Diane keeps them turned down now so that she doesn't have to keep turning them off.

The lights continue to do what they want and footsteps still wander the house at night. Latches go up and down, rustling disturbs the family room, the piano keys randomly play, and a dish will occasionally fall off the kitchen wall and shatter on the counter.

Diane's Black & Decker food chopper disappeared and she has yet to find it.

# 16

## Penn State Mont Alto Campus

**Campus Drive, Mont Alto, Pennsylvania.**

## The Attic

"**S**eems to me these were bedrooms," she said, standing on what remained of the attic floor. Gingerly stepping from one stud to the other on the exposed deck, she had made her way over to one of the windows overlooking the Penn State Mont Alto campus below. Vestiges of what had once been a sturdy floor remained on the perimeter of the space and she positioned herself there so that she could concentrate on what she was "seeing." Half-facing the window and half-facing the room, she continued, "There was a wall down the center of the room. There are bunk beds on each side here, but the room was partitioned and the sides of the attic were separate... Like a dormitory."

Just as had been the case with every other investigation we had conducted, I had told her absolutely nothing about the building we were in or about the stories I had gathered. I had simply picked her up at the prescribed time and brought her here to Wiestling Hall, one of the original buildings on the Mont Alto Campus of the Pennsylvania State University.

Having previously made arrangements with the Chief of Police Services to access Wiestling Hall when it would be closed to students, we had been let into the attic through a padlocked passage by the officer assigned to us. He waited downstairs while we went about our business.

I could well understand why the attic would be padlocked and off-limits. Exposed nails and studs posed danger to the unwary and we had to balance ourselves while avoiding sticky cotton candy-like

insulation that clung to our shoes. Debris from torn down walls and aborted construction covered with years of dust added to the mess. But we were both pretty agile for women in our 50s and had no problem making our way around the hazards.

God knows I had been in my share of attics during my time. I was a retired FBI Supervisory Special Agent and, among many other somewhat unusual assignments, had been trained as a Technical Agent. This meant that for a portion of my career I clandestinely entered buildings or vehicles (with a court order, of course) and bugged them.

My colleague, for want of a better term, was a psychic.

Deborah was working as the children's librarian at the Blue Ridge Summit Library when I met her, having come across her name while doing research for this book. After introducing myself, providing information about my background and project, I asked, "Do you want to look for ghosts?"

"Yes," she replied, "but I've never 'looked' for ghosts."

"Well, you've worked homicide cases, right?"

"Yes."

"And you've located bodies in homicide cases, right?"

"Yes."

I shrugged. "Well, sort of seems like the same thing to me, don't you think?"

She looked at me in an odd sort of way and slowly shook her head. "No... but I'm willing to try it."

That was how we came to find ourselves in the attic of Wiestling Hall—I had taken her there because of the ghost stories circulating for years surrounding

**The attic, Wiestling Hall, Mont Alto.**

Colonel Wiestling and the house he had lived in, which was now named for him. Deborah usually went to the corners of a room first before examining anything else, but once in the attic, she was immediately drawn to one of the windows. I stopped a few feet away and turned on the digital recorder.

"People slept here," she said. Her eyes focused on something I couldn't see and indeed would never see. She called it, "Tuning in." My job was to record what she said and ask questions as they came to mind, and to make sure she didn't trip over anything in this world while attending to the other. "The furnishings are very, very sparse. There might be one very Spartan chest of drawers and two beds." She gestured toward the rest of the attic. "All of this was broken up into little rooms, like dormitory rooms. It feels like people are sleeping all over the place."

She saw no women, just young men. The young men lived there and played cards for entertainment.

"There are no bathrooms up here," she marveled. She saw a washstand and a basin with a little bit of water in it and that was it.

No wonder there were no women, I thought.

Deborah turned her attention outside and looked out the attic window at the Penn State Mont Alto campus below.

She pointed out that there used to be animals on the grounds in a small paddock where the tennis courts are located today; some cows, pigs, and chickens, which were used for food for the people living in Wiestling Hall. "It's like they had a run-in shed or small barn out there for the animals. There might have been a small dairy there, too. Like they made their own butter, milk, cream..." Whoever owned the house essentially "owned" the animals, but did not tend to them. Hired hands took care of that and there were several small structures in the area housing the people who worked there.

Aside from the obvious neglected condition of the attic, Deborah pointed out that the space had not been used for years and that what she was describing had existed sometime during the turn of the last century. "I wouldn't be surprised if people heard footsteps coming from up here," she said.

Deborah had had no way of knowing, as I had not told her and she had conducted no independent research, that the space we were standing in had once been the dormitory for the first public forestry school in the United States.

# Wiestling Hall

The Pennsylvania State Forestry Academy at Mont Alto was founded in 1903. The attic in Wiestling Hall had housed the all-male classes until 1911 when they moved into the new dormitory they had built for themselves, Conklin Hall. The attic was then sealed off and has not been used since.

Wiestling Hall began as a log cabin that was later expanded and covered over with stone. It is the oldest structure in the Penn State University system. Built in 1803, the house originally served as the home of the ironmaster for the Mont Alto Iron Company, founded in 1807 by Daniel, Samuel, and Holker Hughes. The iron ore works occupied the entire Mont Alto campus.

Col. George Wiestling served as commander of the 177th Pennsylvania Emergency Regiment in the Civil War. He suffered wounds that left him partially disabled for the rest of his life, hindering his ability to walk. He bought the Mont Alto Iron Company from the Hughes family in 1864 following his release from the military and moved into the ironmaster's house. In 1889, a gas explosion destroyed the iron ore furnace and caused a huge fire that consumed most of the buildings and equipment, but Wiestling's house was not damaged. The furnace was rebuilt and the Mont Alto Iron Company operated until 1892.

According to an obituary in *The New York Times*, Col. Wiestling died June 17, 1891 in his residence at Mont Alto. The cause of death is listed as "apoplexy," but to some his death is still a mystery. A story passed down among the students suggests that Col. Wiestling shot his mistress and then hanged himself in the attic of his house. As titillating as this story might sound, it is unsupported by historical record.

Wiestling's estate and what remained of the iron works was purchased by the Pennsylvania State Forestry Commission in 1893 and became part of Michaux State Forest. Wiestling's brother and two sisters continued to live in Wiestling Hall until 1903 when the Pennsylvania State Forestry Academy began to train students there and needed the space to house them.

In addition to its role as a dormitory for the first forestry students, Wiestling Hall has served as a dining hall, classroom, and office building. The entire structure, except for the attic, was "modernized" in 2004. Today Wiestling Hall is Mont Alto's Student Center, hosting Student Government Association offices and a cyber café.

## Wiestling's Ghost

Desk and credenza drawers opening and closing, doors flung so hard they'd slam shut, desk chairs spinning, lights turning on and off on their own, and *footsteps, footsteps, footsteps* were common occurrences in the rooms in Wiestling Hall.

When Chancellor Dr. David C. Gnage first reported to the Penn State Mont Alto campus in 2001, his office was on the second floor of Wiestling Hall. He had been warned that, should he find

himself alone in the building late at night, he might hear footsteps coming from the attic above. "Don't worry," he was told. "It's only Col. Wiestling walking around up there."

"Sure enough," Dr. Gnage reported, "I would hear footsteps up there in the evening—after everyone had left the building." The footsteps marched from one end of the attic to the other, increasing in volume and then fading as they moved away.

Other strange things happened as well. The drawers in Dr. Gnage's desk would open and close of their own volition. If he opened a drawer in his credenza and left it, moments later the drawer would suddenly close. And the door to his office would open and close without any visible assistance. He mentioned these inexplicable phenomena to others in Wiestling Hall. "Don't worry about it," they told him. "It's the colonel."

Dr. Gnage recalled a particularly embarrassing episode following his high school reunion in 2003. "At the reunion," he explained, "we were given pins of our high school portraits that had been taken junior year. When I came back to work, I took that pin and threw it in my desk drawer. Later that day, I was speaking to people in my office when the drawer comes open and the picture is sitting there, and all these people I'm talking to see it and laugh." The 60s-style haircut and clothing Dr. Gnage was sporting likely peaked the colonel's curiosity.

Because the colonel appeared so interested in Dr. Gnage's office, he decided to solicit his assistance one evening. "One night I left all my work out with a to-do list. I figured I could have the colonel do it all for me at night." But, alas, when Dr. Gnage opened his office door the following morning, everything on his desk was just as he'd left it. "I guess Civil War ghosts are not computer literate," he lamented.

**Wiestling Hall, Mont Alto.**

Mysterious lights had supposedly been seen in the deserted attic for decades. Campus legend contends that sometime in 1969, when Wiestling Hall was used as a dormitory, a group of students decided to spend the night in the attic, presumably to search for Wiestling's ghost. It was reported that while the students remained in the attic, none of their flashlights would work. However, as soon as the students left the attic, their flashlights operated properly.

People have claimed to hear the sound of hoof beats on the grounds outside of Wiestling Hall. Some believe it's the colonel, astride his horse; others suggest the hoof beats belong to the horses owned by the forestry students, all of whom were required to bring their own.

Dr. Gnage went on to describe a malfunction of the floodlights located on the drive to Wiestling Hall. One night, the lights went out in unison, as if a circuit breaker had been tripped. But *no one*—no one on campus—and none of the electricians hired to solve the problem was able to locate the source of the malfunction. Eventually all of the lights were re-wired and only then did they work. Those familiar with the incident attribute it to Col. Wiestling, suggesting that he did not like the lights on his house, as they were too bright.

When the administrative offices moved to Conklin Hall in 2004, one of the employees transferring to the new location was a former secretary named Kathy who had worked in Wiestling Hall for thirty-five years. The move did not go smoothly, as the telephone service in Conklin Hall malfunctioned and remained dead for days. Once service was restored, fax machines would stop in the middle of a transmission and telephone conversations would be disconnected. "I think the colonel missed Kathy," Dr. Gnage speculated, "and he wanted Kathy to come back to Wiestling."

But the biggest impetus to the belief that Col. Wiestling is still in his house on the Penn State Mont Alto campus is the claim that he appears in a photograph taken of forestry students on their horses in front of Wiestling Hall. Although the photograph in question was taken in 1908, Wiestling, reportedly standing in the background, went unnoticed for decades until a student "discovered" him in the 1980s or 90s.

# Ghostly Occurrences

## *His Domain*

While still in the attic of Wiestling Hall, the word "logging" comes to Deborah's mind and she sees a huge tree being cut down. The people around the tree are preparing to strip the bark off. She doesn't understand why she doesn't see more trees being cut down, but it occurs to her that the people stripping off the bark are actually studying it. "This area was more open then," she said. "The trees have grown in."

Deborah remained standing by the window as she began to describe an ascendant presence. She had felt him from the beginning, but now his status became clear to her. "I can't say he owns this, but he *runs* all this," she said. "He runs this whole property. He's in charge of it. He's the big boss. The superintendent."

"Can you describe him?" I asked.

Deborah began by saying the man has a thick, bushy moustache. "He doesn't have a full face at all, but his cheeks are very red, possibly from exposure to the sun, and he has a bulbous nose." His nondescript brown hair is disheveled and at the time Deborah sees him he does not have a beard. "He is wiry and very outdoorsy. He likes to trek up and down mountains… He's just always out. Like a wood tick. Always out in the woods. He doesn't like to be indoors at all."

I asked Deborah to describe the man's clothes.

"The hat that he's wearing—it's not what I would call a hunting cap, but he's saying it's a hunting cap… It actually looks more like a fishing cap to me… It's a hat and then it has a brim… It looks like a fisherman's cap, the kind they put those lures in." But he keeps telling her it's a hunting cap.

He is wearing pants that resemble knickers. "He looks like he has knee-high socks on and what would be termed boots, but they're ankle length… The pants are loden green and the socks are grey mottled with flecks of white. The socks are wool." Deborah described the pants as being made from the same type of material used by mountain climbers in the Alps in Europe. "It's thick, like moleskin… not boiled wool… moleskin… thick and soft…" The pants appear to have more "give" to them than cotton.

His leather boots are brown and come to ankle length and tie. "They tie in a strange way… They come up around the ankle and do this funny loop thing." But Deborah can't explain it any more clearly than that.

The plaid shirt he is wearing is made from a muslin material that is thick and itchy. "The plaid pattern is green and maroon with a tiny bit of white. It is predominately green and has some beige-grey in it."

The man's brown suede vest has pockets in it and he has a long-barreled rifle with him that looks like a hunting gun.

Deborah wondered why he kept showing her forests. "He keeps saying, 'woods.' He takes care of the woods, too. He oversees what goes on in the woods. There's a lot more property here than just this little area. He keeps showing me trees. Lots of trees. Lots of acreage. And somehow, he is the boss of all this."

Deborah explained that whoever this man was, he felt he was not being paid the appropriate compensation for his work. "He had a great deal of responsibility, but any money that was made did not come to him. He was paid just a regular salary… He believed he was worth more than he was getting… I don't think his wife and children lived very well…"

I asked Deborah if she could get his name…but names rarely come through clearly. She was unsuccessful. She believed this man, at the time she was seeing him, might have been in his 40s, but ages are clouded as well.

"But he is the prevalent energy," Deborah stated. "He is the driving force *here* and this man is all over the place. This whole thing is *his*… This is *his* domain."

### The Second Floor

As we left the attic and began to investigate the second floor, I kept wondering who this man was who dominated all the other energies in the house and grounds. Could it be Wiestling? The description sounded odd for a Civil War colonel, but then I did not know what Wiestling looked like. And Deborah's rule was that no information was to be provided until she was finished. This way, nothing she "saw" was contaminated. So I could not suggest the name, nor could I pose questions containing information.

Deborah did not like the second floor. She sensed that the floor had originally consisted of five large rooms and most had been "cut up" into smaller rooms and offices. The air was thin and stuffy in some of the smaller rooms and Deborah found it difficult to breathe…it was as if the house were wounded and gasping for breath.

But in an office in a room that had not been altered too much, Deborah was able to relax...and she saw a small girl there, playing by the window.

Deborah described the girl as between six and eight years old and wearing a robin's egg blue dress made of material that is "not stiff and it's not shiny like satin... It's a step up from cotton... The dress has puffy little sleeves and lots of lace around the ends of the sleeves and the collar..." Although it's a nice dress, this girl's family is not wealthy. A matching blue bow adorns her long, reddish-blonde hair. There is a ruddiness to her complexion as if she spends a lot of time playing outside in the sun.

She might be related in some way to the gentleman in the attic, or she might not be a part of his era at all. From her dress it appears she might be from the early 1900s. There are three boys associated with her who were likely her brothers. Spaced around two years apart in age, two of the boys are older than she is and the youngest boy appears to have just learned how to walk.

"She likes to make her presence known," Deborah said. "She likes to look out the windows here and she likes to open doors. She doesn't do anything bad. She just likes to be around the windows... I would not be surprised if someone were sitting in here working or whatever, and one of these chairs swings around by itself."

We continued our examination of the second floor. Deborah commented, "The gentleman upstairs is not happy about this," referring to the alterations in the house. "He's not happy about any of it."

### "She is not happy."

A woman is present with the children, but she does not interact with them and it isn't clear what her relationship is to the man who runs the grounds. Impressions suggest she is his wife, but this is not clear. She might be the wife of another who lived here at one time. What is clear is that this woman is very unhappy.

Whoever she is, this woman is very non-confrontational and, although she makes her displeasure known to her husband in subtle ways, she will not come right out and tell him that she wants to leave. She knows he would never tolerate this. There is no way she is going to get away from here until he is ready to go himself. Deborah sensed that this woman "did not grow up anywhere around here. She's from relatively far away and she is not happy that her husband got the 'post' here. She's not happy about living in this area and she wants to go home."

Later, in the basement, Deborah sensed that this woman tended to a root cellar or similar area. "She's standing over there," Deborah said, pointing to the corner of the room where the original outline of Wiestling Hall's foundation can still be seen. "There are plants and bulbs in that corner. She keeps them there until they are ready to be planted. She comes down here to can things, too. She spends time in this basement."

Deborah described her as being incredibly plain. "There's no spark to her," Deborah elaborated. "She's not a person you would remember if you ever saw her."

She is approximately five feet two to three inches tall. She has a pasty complexion and her drab brown hair is pulled back into a disheveled bun. She is wearing a plain blue shirtwaist dress from the early 1900s that flares out slightly and just hangs on her thin frame. Her glossy leather boots, dark brown and sporting a tiny heel, are out of place with the dress, but seem to be the only pair of shoes she owns. She rarely speaks, but when she does, her soft voice is barely audible. Although she finds solace in her garden, a tiny patch she tends just outside the house, it is nowhere near enough to soothe her gloom. "She is not happy," Deborah said. "She's just existing."

Still on the second floor, we then entered one of the larger rooms, next to a back stairway from the main floor below, and Deborah stated without hesitation, "Someone died in this room."

## Sarah Hurley Matheny

By the time Sarah Hurley Matheny was twenty-nine years old and employed for the second time as a kitchen worker for the Pennsylvania State Forest Academy, she had already been deserted by her husband and had lived with and left William Reed. According to someone interviewed at the time of her death, Sarah Hurley Matheny "was a charming woman who loved not wisely but too well."

Matheny had first met William Reed when he worked as a contractor for a company involved with the Forest Academy some months prior. Once they became involved with one another, Matheny quit her job at the Forest Academy and went to live with Reed. But the relationship soured, and Matheny eventually left Reed and returned to work and live at Wiestling Hall. Matheny did, however, continue to see Reed on the weekends.

At approximately 9:15 a.m. on the morning of May 9, 1911, Matheny was alone in the kitchen in Wiestling Hall, apparently grinding coffee, when an intoxicated Reed appeared outside the door to the kitchen and demanded to see her. He later claimed he was there to demand she turn over some personal papers of his she had in her possession that included his discharge papers from the Spanish-American War and some photographs. Matheny reportedly made two trips to her room on the second floor of Wiestling Hall to retrieve Reed's documents, but threw them into the kitchen's wood stove instead of turning them over. Then she raised the coffee grinder as if to throw it at him and demanded that Reed leave.

Reed took out his revolver and shot her twice, hesitated, and then shot her once more.

Several Forest Academy employees heard the shots and came upon the scene within seconds. As Reed calmly walked away, Matheny, blood pouring from her wounds and gasping for breath, was carried upstairs to her bedroom. She died almost immediately.

Many people who saw and spoke to Reed that day immediately after the murder testified at his trial that Reed clearly admitted to the shooting and had even turned himself in to a constable who happened to be his uncle. Reed, although acknowledging he had killed Matheny, pleaded not guilty to a first-degree murder charge, claiming that while he had meant to fire the revolver at Matheny, he had not meant to kill her.

When asked by a reporter during the trial why, if Reed claimed that killing Matheny was an accident, had he shot her a third time, Reed responded, "I didn't think the first two shots had hit her."

Matheny had been struck by all three bullets and, according to the autopsy report, the third shot had been the fatal round. The bullet had entered her side, passed through her heart, and exited her chest. The trajectory indicated that Matheny had been turned away from Reed when she was struck, likely fleeing from him after being shot in the neck and face.

On Sunday, September 10, 1911, the jury returned a verdict of guilty of murder in the first degree.

Reed was held at the Old Jail on King Street in Chambersburg following his conviction. He was held in a section of the jail used to house female prisoners so as to keep the condemned man away from the rest of the prison population. Reed remained calm and self-possessed throughout his incarceration—up until the moment of his execution.

According to an article in *The Franklin Repository*, a Chambersburg newspaper, dated April 30, 1912, the prisoners held a service for

Reed the night before his execution. One Jack Ross from California, reportedly a "college graduate and well-connected, in jail for stealing when drunk," called all the men together and told them he thought they should conduct a service. The men held their service in the corridor of the men's quadrant of the jail. As Reed was walked out to the gallows the next morning, he allegedly called goodbye to the women working in the jail kitchen and to the prisoners he passed in their cells.

William Reed was executed April 30, 1912 on the gallows at the Old Jail in Chambersburg, Pennsylvania. Newspaper sources reported that the "drop" fell at 10:06 a.m., and Reed was pronounced dead at 10:16 a.m. Reed would become the last man executed by hanging in Franklin County. The day was summed up in one notable newspaper observation: "A more successful execution was never seen in Pennsylvania."

For decades afterward, until Wiestling Hall was renovated and the old kitchen disappeared into new construction, workers complained of appliances coming on by themselves, such as a potato peeler that seemed to have a mind of its own, pots and pans banging together on shelves, and hooks disturbed by unseen hands. It's alleged that to this day, bloodstains appear on the stairway leading from the old kitchen area on the first floor of Wiestling Hall to the second floor bedroom where Matheny died. The stains appear as blackish marks in the wood steps, but disappear shortly after being noticed. And wails that emanate from the dark room at night where she was carried mortally wounded are thought to be Matheny's dying cries.

## *The Chancellor's Old Office*

We entered the office once occupied by the chancellor. The entity first sensed in the attic continued to provide information. Deborah sat on a couch in the room and said that the gentleman from the attic "would rifle through things because he wants to know what's going on in his area. He might actually open a file cabinet and leave it open just to worry people. He just wants to check out what's going on."

I recalled what Dr. Gnage had told me about the goings-on in his office. It all seemed to make sense now. This entity, whoever he was, had once been in charge and acts as if he's still in charge. Naturally he would want to see what the chancellor was up to. I wondered if the faculty member currently occupying the office suffered similar intrusions.

"He keeps talking about the Alps," Deborah said. "The mountains. He wants to show me something that has to do with the mountains. The 'Alps' keeps coming to me."

Wondering if it was the colonel, I asked Deborah to ask the entity if he had been in any wars.

She paused and then said, "He won't say yes or no. He keeps showing me mountains. He keeps saying something about climbing mountains. Something to do with the Alps."

This man was everywhere.

## The First Floor

Although original logs can be seen along the wall in the seating area of the student center and the outer walls and underlying foundation remain in place, little on the first floor is recognizable as the old Wiestling Hall. While the first floor is now very practical, suited to a modern campus and the needs and wants of current students, the gutting of the infrastructure dissipated any energy that might have found solace in familiar surroundings. "There's nothing here," Deborah said. We stood in the seating area for the cyber café. The air felt vacant and still. Sterile. She looked at me and said, "The house has been brutalized."

There was only one room, a large room with a fireplace just inside the front entrance, where energies linger. Other than inserting a soft drink machine and a pool table, it appeared as if the room had not been seriously assaulted. Even the large, oversized heavy wooden door leading to the adjacent room, now a storage closet, had managed to escape replacement.

Deborah sat on a chair here and said, "It's dark. There's a fire going. Gas lights. Doesn't look like it's electricity, but I don't see candles sitting around." Deborah indicated there was a lot of people in the room, all men, some of whom were smoking pipes. It seemed to her this was a reception room of some sort because it didn't look like the people in the room were having a party and there were too many of them to be members of the same family. "The atmosphere is more like a lodge," she said. "Nothing here is fancy."

"This is where people came to be indoctrinated," Deborah continued. "Orientation. There's a little bit of food, but it's not a party atmosphere. This is what's going to be expected of you, et cetera. This is what you're going to do, et cetera... It's a happy thing. It's where people congregate. This is probably the warmest room in the house from an emotional standpoint. It's happy and hopeful. It's a hopeful room. It's almost an idealistic room. Like people here talk about plans they're going to make and things that are going to happen."

And the man from the attic was here, too. "This is not a religious place at all," Deborah said. "People don't pray here. It's almost as if that man—he thinks that nature is his religion, as opposed to praying to a God. He thinks that nature is proof that there is a God... This is a good room."

## Who Was the Man in the Attic?

More than two hours had passed and we were both tired. It had been a long day—but the mystery had not been solved. I asked the campus police officer that had accompanied us if there were any place on campus where we could look at photographs of people who had worked or lived in Wiestling Hall. He directed us toward the General Studies Building.

A huge glass-enclosed display case loaded with black and white photographs greeted us on the wall just inside the entrance. "Do you think you would recognize him if you saw his picture?" I asked Deborah. She had already begun to scan the images. "Yes," she replied. Up and down she looked, carefully studying each photograph, moving slowly from one row to the next. I just stood there, watching. Finally, she got to the last row.

"That's him!" she exclaimed.

"Where?"

She pointed to the first picture in the row, in the upper right-hand corner of the display case. "That's him! Look at his face! Look at that cap! I told you it looked like a fisherman's cap!"

We were both too far away to read the name under the picture. I looked around and dragged over a chair that had been sitting in the hallway. I climbed up on it to see the name.

"That's him!" Deborah said again, proud of her discovery. "Who is he?"

I couldn't believe I was looking at a photograph of a man wearing a hunting cap that looked like a fisherman's cap—*just as Deborah had described*—along with the face she had detailed, style of clothing, and even the correct rifle. I read the name. It wasn't Wiestling. "It's Rothrock," I said. "Somebody Rothrock."

"Who's Rothrock?" Deborah asked.

I shrugged. "I have no idea."

# Joseph Trimble Rothrock
# (1839-1922)

Joseph Trimble Rothrock was born April 9, 1839 in McVeytown, Pennsylvania. His grandfather, a farmer, had migrated from Germany a generation before and had passed down to his sons and their sons a deep appreciation and respect for nature and the environment.

The beauty of Pennsylvania's forests struck Rothrock at a relatively young age. After attending Tuscarora Academy of Academia in Juniata County as a youth and being captivated by the beauty of the setting, Rothrock later purchased the academy's lands. The site eventually became Rothrock State Forest.

Rothrock then attended Freeland Seminary (now Ursinus College) in Montgomery County, Pennsylvania. He subsequently earned a Bachelor of Science degree in botany from Harvard University in 1862 where he studied under renowned botanist Asa Grey.

The outbreak of the Civil War halted Rothrock's pursuits and he enlisted in the Union Army on July 1, 1863. Eventually attaining the rank of captain in the 20th Pennsylvania Calvary, Rothrock was seriously wounded at the Battle of Fredericksburg. His military service ended on June 6, 1864.

The end of the war allowed Rothrock to continue his studies and he went on to obtain his medical degree from the University of Pennsylvania in 1867. Rothrock then became a professor of botany, human anatomy, and physiology at the Agricultural College of Pennsylvania (now the Pennsylvania State University) from 1867 to 1869.

Rothrock married Martha E. May of West Chester, Pennsylvania, on May 27, 1868, and the couple moved to Wilkes-Barre in 1869 where Rothrock practiced medicine and eventually helped to found the Wilkes-Barre Hospital.

Like the "wood tick" he was compared to, Rothrock couldn't seem to stand still long enough to pursue just one of his interests. In 1865 and 1873, he went on exploratory expeditions to British Columbia and unsettled regions of the western United States, serving as a botanist and surgeon. In 1873 Rothrock began concentrating on botanical research and served as the primary botanist for the United States Engineers until 1875.

Rothrock then took a professorship with the University of Pennsylvania where he taught botany and became a faculty member in the Department of Medicine.

Rothrock's concentration on forestry began to fully reveal itself when he was appointed the Michaux Lecturer for the promotion of botany and forestry in 1877. Rothrock had been following and attempting to call attention to the deforestation of Pennsylvania's land for years. The end of the Civil War brought an unprecedented increase in the demand for lumber while iron companies consumed acres of trees on a daily basis to fire their

DR. ROTHROCK ON INDIAN ROCKS.

furnaces. Absolutely no attempt was being made to replace the trees and what had once been stunning landscapes protected by thick canopies were evolving into miles of barren hills that threatened mudslides with every rain. Having traveled extensively in the United States, Rothrock went to Germany in 1880 where he studied botany at the University of Strasburg. While there, he visited the forests of Europe and gathered information on Europe's forest management programs.

Rothrock's efforts prompted the Commonwealth to act, and in 1886, Rothrock was elected president of the newly

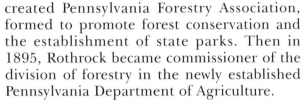

created Pennsylvania Forestry Association, formed to promote forest conservation and the establishment of state parks. Then in 1895, Rothrock became commissioner of the division of forestry in the newly established Pennsylvania Department of Agriculture.

Rothrock was the driving force behind the establishment of the Pennsylvania Forest Academy at Mont Alto. In 1904, Rothrock resigned as commissioner of forestry, but continued to serve as a commission member until 1914 when he resigned due to ill health. He died June 2, 1922 in West Chester, Pennsylvania, at the age of eighty-three.

It's likely Rothrock would have achieved great notoriety and fame as a botanist in his time had he not dedicated the later portion of his life to forestry. He had already achieved national recognition as a botanist, but by refocusing his attention when he did, he effectively destroyed any possibility of truly distinguishing fame. Most of Rothrock's recognition was achieved in the years following his death when the impact of the programs he put into place began to be better appreciated.

**Photograph of Dr. Joseph T. Rothrock identified by Deborah Heinecker in Mont Alto display.**
*Original photograph courtesy and © of Becky Dietrich.*

Rothrock eventually became known as the "Father of Pennsylvania Forestry." While it's a well-deserved and defining title, his name to this day is much less known than that of another Civil War veteran whose life's achievements have long since disappeared, but who is recognized and spoken of by generations of Penn State Mont Alto students simply because it is believed he haunts the house named after him.

# Epilogue

People will continue to speak of odd occurrences in Wiestling Hall. Tradition will trounce alternative theories and a true photographic analysis of the only purported evidence of Wiestling's presence will never be conducted, but this is as it should be.

The beauty of any ghost story is that it can never be proved or disproved. The tale is there to be told in whatever light the teller wishes to cast.

This teller chooses to cast the glow on Rothrock.

It isn't Col. Wiestling who haunts Wiestling Hall. It's Rothrock. Rothrock is the pervasive energy dominating the structure, throwing open cabinet drawers, and looking through the papers and desks of current occupants. Rothrock is the one who turns lights on and off in vacant rooms and causes electronic equipment to malfunction when displeased. Rothrock's restless footsteps are the ones heard coming from the attic, along with the footsteps of the first Forestry Academy students.

Rothrock is everywhere. After all, Mont Alto is *his* domain.

~~~~~~~

**Dr. Joseph T. Rothrock.** *Courtesy and © of Becky Dietrich.*

# The Zouave Photographs

## A Surprising Climax

Deborah was restless and for some odd reason decided that she wanted to visit Gettysburg.

"Are you insane?" I asked her. "You remember what happened the last time you went there?"

A few years back, Deborah had reluctantly agreed to accompany visiting friends on one of Gettysburg's many ghost walks. The tour wound through the town and at one point paused at the entrance of a church where the guide recounted a tragic tale. Deborah sat down on the steps as the guide spoke...and felt a piercing blow to her chest and suddenly discovered that she could not breathe. She had inadvertently alighted on the very spot where the subject of the guide's tale had been shot and killed.

She shrugged. "I want to visit the battlefield. So long as I don't sit down where anyone was killed I should be fine."

"Great," I said. "The ladies room in the visitor's center would probably be the only safe place."

The summer night was falling as we drove onto the battlefield. The air had cooled and the sky had taken on a warm orange glow from the disappearing sun. We entered at Pleasonton Avenue and made a right turn onto Hancock Avenue. The battlefield spread toward the horizon on our left while cars abandoned by tourists occupied most of the parking spaces on our right. Spying an opening, Deborah announced, "Pull over here."

I slid my car into the open space. Deborah and I got out of the car and started to walk toward the ridge. Markers and monuments commemorating the soldiers who fought there dotted the landscape. A display next to the road explained that this location represented the "High Water Mark" of the war. Tourists meandered toward the sunset, attempting to capture the gloaming on their digital cameras and cell phones.

Gettysburg monument honoring the 72$^{nd}$ Pennsylvania Volunteer Infantry Philadelphia Fire Zouaves.... *Deborah's* Zouave.

Deborah suddenly turned left. "I want to go this way," she said, heading for a cluster of monuments dotting the ridge.

I had learned by this time not to ask, but to simply follow. I glanced ahead of her at the monuments and saw *him* immediately, rifle raised in battle, his billowy pants silhouetted in the orange sky. "It's a Zouave!" I yelled, disturbing everyone around us and running past her toward the monument.

"No it's not," Deborah said. She knew that she had been drawn there, yet didn't know why.

"Yes it is! Look at him!"

"Well…so *it* is."

He stood atop the monument dedicated to the 72$^{nd}$ Pennsylvania Volunteer Philadelphia Fire Zouaves. Other than the cap, the statue wore clothing almost identical to those worn by the self-possessed fellow Deborah had "seen" in the Toll House.

I walked all around the monument, taking pictures from different angles until the sun gradually slipped away.

"How do you do that?" I asked, shaking my head.

"I have no idea," Deborah replied. Out of all the monuments in Gettysburg, Deborah had somehow been led to this one. "Obviously someone wanted me to see this statue."

"It has to be the Zouave in the Toll House."

"But why? Why would he want me to come here?"

Then the answer to the mystery became clear. "He was jealous," I said. "He wanted to show you how important he was. He was probably annoyed that we were talking about Rothrock all day."

# Bibliography

Arthur, Don and Ron Keiper. *Renfrew Park*. Waynesboro, Pennsylvania: Self-published, 1987.

Dietrich, Becky. *Mont Alto Sampler*. Chambersburg, Pennsylvania: Self-published, 2005.

Guiley, Rosemary Ellen. *The Encyclopedia of Ghosts and Spirits, Second Edition*. New York City, New York: Checkmark Books, 2000.

Heinecker, Deborah M. *The Reluctant Psychic*. Philadelphia, Pennsylvania: Xlibris Corporation, 2000.

Longacre, Judith Evans. *The History of Wilson College 1868 to 1970, Volume 1*. Lewiston, New York: The Edwin Mellon Press, Ltd, 1997.

Marotte, Maurice Leonard, III and Janet Kay Pollard. *Images of America: Chambersburg*. Charleston, South Carolina: Arcadia Publishing, 2005.

Marotte, Maurice Leonard, III and Janet Kay Pollard. *Images of America: Franklin County*. Charleston, South Carolina: Arcadia Publishing, 2007.

Shockey, Bonnie A. and Kenneth B. Shockey. *Images of America: Greencastle-Antrim*. Portsmouth, New Hampshire: Arcadia Publishing, 2004.

*Images of America: Greencastle-Antrim Revisited*. Charleston, South Carolina: Arcadia Publishing, 2007.

Thompson, David W. *Images of America: Around Waynesboro*. Portsmouth, New Hampshire: Arcadia Publishing, 2003.

Woodring, Franklin P. and Suzanne K. Woodring. *Images of America: Pen Mar*. Charleston, South Carolina: Arcadia Publishing, 2005.

## Websites

Answers.com: accessed July 4, 2008 at www.answers.com/topic/ zouave.

"Anthony Wayne, Man of Action" at Pennsylvania Historical and Museum Commission: accessed July 7, 2008 at www.phmc.state. pa.us/ppet/wayne/page1.as?secid=31.

"Battle of Fallen Timbers": accessed July 4, 2008 at www. ohiohistorycentral.org/entry.php?rec=473.

"Borough of Waynesboro": accessed July 7, 2008 at www.waynesboropa. org/history1.htm.

http://www.philazou.home.mindspring.com/page2.html; July 4, 2008

http://www.zouave.org/; July 4, 2008

Harrington, Hugh T., and Lisa A. Ennis. "'Mad' Anthony Wayne, His Body Did Not Rest In Peace." Americanrevolution.org; accessed November 2, 2007 at http://americanrevolution.org/ wayne.html.

http://www.nationalroadpa.org/historical_timeline.html; March 25, 2008.

http://www/lhhc.org/content/subpage/hist.html; March 21, 2008.

"Was Gen. 'Mad Anthony' Wayne Really Mad?" Ushistory.org; accessed July 7, 2008 at http://www.ushistory.org/paoli/history/waynemad. html.

"Wayne Buried in Two Places." Ushistory.org; accessed November 7, 2007 at http://www.ushistory.org/paoli/history/wayneburied. html.

"Who Served Here?" Ushistory.org; November 7, 2007 at http://www. ushistory.org/valleyforge/served/wayne.html.